# got data?
## NOW WHAT?

*Creating and Leading*
*Cultures of Inquiry*

# LAURA LIPTON • BRUCE WELLMAN

Solution Tree | Press

a division of
Solution Tree

555 North Morton Street
Bloomington, IN 47404
800.733.6786 (toll free) / 812.336.7700
FAX: 812.336.7790

email: info@solution-tree.com
solution-tree.com

Visit **go.solution-tree.com/teams** to download the reproducibles in this book.

Printed in the United States of America

16   15                    8   9   10

Library of Congress Cataloging-in-Publication Data

Lipton, Laura.
   Got data? now what? : creating and leading cultures of inquiry / Laura Lipton, Bruce Wellman.
       p. cm.
   Includes bibliographical references and index.
   ISBN 978-1-936765-03-4 (perfect bound) -- ISBN 978-1-936765-04-1 (library edition)
1.  Educational statistics. 2.  Group work in education.  I. Wellman, Bruce M. II. Title.
   LB2846.L55 2012
   370.21--dc23
                              2011050649

**Solution Tree**
Jeffrey C. Jones, CEO
Edmund M. Ackerman, President

**Solution Tree Press**
*President:* Douglas M. Rife
*Publisher:* Robert D. Clouse
*Vice President of Production:* Gretchen Knapp
*Managing Production Editor:* Caroline Wise
*Copy Editor:* Sarah Payne-Mills
*Proofreader:* Elisabeth Abrams
*Text and Cover Designer:* Jenn Taylor

# Acknowledgments

We extend our appreciation for the warm welcome from the Solution Tree team, and the care, attention, and respect given to our work during the production of this book. We are grateful to the researchers and authors whose thinking and writing have inspired and informed us. The reference section of this book is a tribute to them. We are appreciative of the many teachers and administrators who joined us in the learning process, shared their successes and dilemmas, and made these practices their own. Finally, we could not have created this book without the patience and support of our MiraVia team members, especially graphic artist Michael Buckley, who created many of the original figures in this book. Their willingness to adjust to our work schedule is a tribute to their flexibility and dedication.

Solution Tree Press would like to thank the following reviewers:

Deborah DiPrato
Second-Grade Teacher
Sand Lake Elementary
Orlando, Florida

Susan Huff
Principal
Spanish Oaks Elementary
Spanish Fork, Utah

Angela Linker
English Language Arts
  Department Chair
Madison High School
Vienna, Virginia

Janet Malone
PLC at Work™ Associate
Solution Tree
Encinitas, California

Randall W. Peterson
Principal
Eastview High School
Apple Valley, Minnesota

Sarah Schuhl
PLC at Work™ Associate
Solution Tree
Gresham, Oregon

Darwin Prater Spiller
Principal
Stults Road Elementary
Dallas, Texas

Visit **go.solution-tree.com/teams** to download
the reproducibles in this book.

# Table of Contents

*Reproducible pages are in italics.*

# *About the Authors*

LAURA LIPTON, EdD, is codirector of MiraVia. Laura is an international consultant whose writing, research, and seminars focus on implementing effective and innovative instructional practices and on building professional and organizational capacities for enhanced learning. Laura engages with schools and school districts, designing and conducting workshops on learning-focused instruction, literacy development, and strategies to support beginning teachers. She facilitates organizational adaptivity and learning through training and development in data-driven dialogue, group development, action research, and learning-focused collaborations.

Laura is the author and coauthor of numerous publications related to organizational and professional development, learning-focused schools, and literacy development. Her selected publications include *Groups at Work: Strategies and Structures for Professional Learning, More Than 50 Ways to Learner-Centered Literacy* (second edition), *Data-Driven Dialogue: A Facilitator's Guide to Collaborative Inquiry, Making Mentoring Work: An ASCD Action Tool, Mentoring Matters: A Practical Guide to Learning-Focused Relationships* (second edition), and *Pathways to Understanding: Patterns and Practices in the Learning-Focused Classroom* (third edition).

Laura has been a featured speaker at international, national, and state conferences since 1984. She has shared her expertise with thousands of educators throughout North America, as well as Central America, Asia, Australia, and New Zealand. To learn more about Laura's work, visit www.miravia.com or follow @lelipton on Twitter.

BRUCE WELLMAN is codirector of MiraVia. He consults with school systems, professional groups, and organizations throughout North America, and he presents on the patterns and practices of learning-focused classrooms, learning-focused conversations, effective presentation skills, and facilitation and development of collaborative groups.

Bruce is an award-winning writer whose work has been honored by the Education Writers Association and Learning Forward. He is the author and coauthor of numerous publications related to organizational and professional development, mentoring, quality teaching, and improving professional cultures.

His selected publications include *Groups at Work: Strategies and Structures for Professional Learning, Data-Driven Dialogue: A Facilitator's Guide to Collaborative Inquiry, Learning-Focused Mentoring: A Professional Development Resource Kit, Mentoring Matters: A Practical Guide to Learning-Focused Relationships, Pathways to Understanding: Patterns and Practices in the Learning-Focused Classroom, The Adaptive School: A Sourcebook for Developing Collaborative Groups,* and *How to Make Presentations That Teach and Transform.*

Bruce has served as a classroom teacher, curriculum coordinator, and staff developer in Oberlin, Ohio, and Concord, Massachusetts, public schools. He holds a bachelor's degree from Antioch College and a master's of education from Lesley College. To learn more about Bruce's work, visit www.miravia.com or follow @brucewellman on Twitter.

To book Laura or Bruce for professional development, contact pd@solution-tree .com.

# *Introduction*

• • • • • • • • • • • • • • • • • • • • • • • • • • • • • • • • • • • • • • • •

It is 3:15 p.m., and several members of the fourth-grade team at Gardenview Elementary are late, as usual, for the scheduled 3:00 p.m. meeting. They eventually straggle in, some with the materials for exploration, some without. Those without their class rubrics need to go back to their classrooms to retrieve them. After a few greetings and a few grumbles, the conversation gets started.

This week's facilitator suggests the members look at the student results for word choice based on the rubric they constructed for expository writing.

"My class was all over the place in this skill set, how about yours?"

"My kids didn't do very well. I think we should create word walls in every classroom to build vocabulary."

"Before we do that, I think we should create some common vocabulary lesson plans."

"Yeah, but we should include word walls in them."

"And then we could give another assignment to see if the results are the same."

"Why do we need to teach exactly the same way? I'd like to do more integrated vocabulary building, and we're not all teaching the same social studies or science units."

The facilitator struggles for the group's attention and says, "Wait, before we start fixing, we should look at all the rubrics."

But at that point, the clock strikes 4:00, and the meeting adjourns.

• • • • • • • • • • • • • • • • • • • • • • • • • • • • • • • • • • • • • • • •

This group, like many struggling groups, is limited by its lack of structure, shared goals, and skill with collaborative analysis of data. Such teams flounder because they try to operate without protocols and because they lack the communication skills for managing sensitive conversations about student learning and current teaching practices. Often they are trapped by a narrow definition of data as test, state, or provincial scores, and as a result, the types of data they examine constrain rich, collaborative conversations and important discoveries about student growth. These data are too far from the local classroom and individual learners to stimulate powerful conversations about practice. Unfortunately, the pressure to produce growth—growth as measured by these scores in particular—drives the team to limit its collaborative conversations to these high-stakes data sources. Pressured groups then focus on targeted interventions and test-taking skills to move a few students from one level of proficiency to the next, not on developing deep changes that produce rich learning for all.

# The Promises and Problems of Collaborative Cultures

As in the opening scenario, school teams confront three common dilemmas in their work with data. These dilemmas present technical, personal, and social challenges for individual group members and for the group as a whole: (1) committee without community, (2) time without tools, and (3) data without deliberation.

## Committee Without Community

Being in the room doesn't mean individuals necessarily identify as members of the group or think of themselves as interlocking parts of the whole. Professional identity as a solo practitioner conflicts with a sense of collective responsibility for student learning and a commitment to collaborative exploration of data, options, and actions. Student results as a shared responsibility and instructional repertoire as a common toolkit are radical notions for teachers who view their primary workplace as the classroom and not the school.

Group members avoid tough-to-talk-about topics when they lack the relational skills to manage the mental and emotional demands of improving student learning. Moving from *my students* and *my work* to *our students* and *our work* requires clear purpose, safe structures, and compelling data that present vivid images of the effects of teachers' work. This shift from individual perspective to collective perspective is the heart of collaborative inquiry as teacher teams search for the patterns and practices that produce learning success for all students.

> *Moving from* my students *and* my work *to* our students *and* our work *requires clear purpose, safe structures, and compelling data that present vivid images of the effects of teachers' work.*

## Time Without Tools

Structural change is not cultural change. Simply altering the schedule to provide time to meet does not create conditions for learning or increase enthusiasm for the demands of collaborative engagement. Protected time without productive use builds resentment when group members feel that they are being kept from their real work back in the classroom.

Front-loaded training is a necessary but insufficient resource for developing fluency and confidence with the skills of collaborative inquiry. To institutionalize patterns of thoughtful practice requires the group's ongoing attention to goal setting, self-assessment, collective assessment, reflection, and redirection.

## Data Without Deliberation

Data-rich environments in and of themselves do not produce robust improvements in instructional practice and student learning. Milbrey McLaughlin (2011) suggests:

> *A significant obstacle to the collaborative, ongoing, and frank discussions about*
> *data and student progress found in strong teacher learning communities lies in*
> *teachers' general lack of knowledge about how to understand the data available to*
> *them, how to develop assessments of student progress specific to their classrooms,*
> *and how to link data to action. (p. 67)*

Collaborative inquiry is complex and often stretches the capacities of many groups. When group members do not embrace a spirit of inquiry, habits of judgment and critique constrain both group growth and effective problem solving. As a result of these limitations, groups tend to simplify problems and apply narrow solutions, rather than embrace the messiness of tenacious issues.

Collaborative inquiry is a value as much as it is a skill set. Its true value emerges from the daily disciplines of practice, persistence, and attention to process. Skilled data use influences group development, and simultaneously, group development influences skilled data use. Patient and thoughtful groups learn to trust the process, their data, and one another.

High-performing teams systematically collect and use data to drive cycles of problem solving, planning, action, and reflection to both improve their own collaborative practices and improve instruction that makes a difference in student learning. Conversely, when teachers work in isolation without the grounding that data or collegial perspectives provide, they tend to rely on habit and make decisions based on anecdotal evidence and intuition. Some of the literature in the field of group development (see, for example, DuFour, DuFour, Eaker, & Many, 2010) makes distinctions between the terms *groups* and *teams* and *collegial* and *collaborative*. In this book, we use these terms interchangeably to refer to professional communities that share common goals and view each other as resources for exploring practice and improving learning, using data to inform their conversations and decisions.

Although the power of data-driven collaboration is well researched (see for example, Louis & Marks, 1998; McLaughlin & Talbert, 2001) it is often difficult to establish as a norm in schools. As DuFour et al. (2010) remind us, "A collaborative culture does not simply emerge in a school or district: leaders cultivate collaborative cultures when they develop the capacity of their staffs to work as members of high-performing teams" (p. 153).

## What You'll Find in This Book

*Got Data? Now What? Creating and Leading Cultures of Inquiry* is a practical and accessible resource for confronting these dilemmas. It provides the strategies and tools for deep and deliberate work with data that turn struggling committees into powerful communities of learners. It is intended for group leaders—including instructional coaches, department chairs, team leaders, building and district administrators, and group members—who want meaningful and time-efficient work sessions that produce greater learning for all.

*Got Data? Now What?* draws from our work with professional learning communities, data teams, and grade-level, department, and administrative meetings. This book shares the lessons we've learned and presents practical, time-efficient methods for effectively completing tasks while developing productive collaborative relationships.

This book is based on the following five assumptions about group leadership.

1.  **Assessment and feedback drive group growth:** Group development is an active ongoing process, not a result.

2.  **Group development and task accomplishment intertwine:** Groups need purposeful structures and practical tools to learn with and from their data and one another.

3.  **When groups change the way they talk, they change the way they work:** Thoughtful, systematic data-driven exploration of the results of instructional practice produces learning gains for both students and teachers.

4.  **Comfort with discomfort is necessary for collaborative learning:** Willingness to navigate the emotional challenges of work with data is a key factor for group success.

5.  **Patterns become habits, habits become norms, and norms shape behavior:** The real goal is to positively influence the culture of the organization. High-performing groups are vehicles for producing high-performing cultures, not an end in themselves.

We present a three-phase learning cycle—the collaborative learning cycle—which is a framework for using data to energize collaborative practices that improve student learning. Each chapter offers concepts, tools, tips, exercises, and a data story that illuminates the central focus. Each chapter also offers an Exercise Your Learning section with opportunities for application of the information in the chapter and an Extend Your Learning section with additional resources for further exploration. Visit **go.solution-tree.com/teams** to download the reproducibles and access the links in this book.

Chapter 1 presents the traits of high-performing data cultures and ways to purposefully develop and sustain learner-centered practices in schools. We offer an inventory for turning these standards of excellence into data for feedback and self-correction to produce ongoing improvements in group performance. The data story illustrates an elementary group applying data about its processes and interactions to refine and improve collaborative skills.

Chapter 2 presents a three-phase, inquiry-driven model for guiding productive group work with data—the collaborative learning cycle. Examples of purpose, process, potential, and pitfalls elaborate each phase of the model. We offer applications and tips for success, and we emphasize the importance of structuring group work and the liabilities that occur when scaffolds and skills are missing. The data story illustrates the collaborative learning cycle in action as a middle school team works with data from a benchmark expository writing assessment.

Chapter 3 presents ways to frame issues for investigation. These fundamental choices direct a group's attention and data pursuits. We describe how expert groups use structured inquiry to identify gaps and successes and to clarify root causes before generating solutions. The data story illustrates a high school language arts team grappling with student performance gaps in reading comprehension of informational texts.

Chapter 4 presents fundamental definitions and descriptions of data types and uses with tips and cautions for choosing and using effective data displays. We offer approaches for data gathering including data that are presently available or archival and data that might need to be collected via constructed tools such as surveys or interviews. The data story illustrates an elementary math coach helping a vertical team consider possible causes for gaps in student problem-solving skills and identify formative assessment data to explore the issue.

Chapter 5 presents the group-member knowledge, skills, and dispositions that drive high performance. We describe stages of group development including predictable challenges, developmental indicators, and requirements for transitioning from one stage to the next. The data story illustrates a middle school team working with a group-development inventory to assess its growth as a team.

Chapter 6 presents distinctions between three essential modes of discourse in data-based conversations: (1) dialogue, (2) discussion, and (3) decision making. We describe common constraints to productive discourse and identify problematic and productive elements in six decision-making methods. The data story illustrates a middle school team applying effective discourse patterns within the collaborative learning cycle to improve a new behavior management program.

Chapter 7 presents approaches for turning decisions into productive plans for action driven by clear and measurable goals. We offer ten tips for avoiding common planning problems and addressing barriers to effectiveness. The data story illustrates a high school science team moving from making a decision to crafting an action plan for improving student inquiry skills across the science curriculum.

## The Road to Learning

School improvement is not easy and quick. Data-driven change requires the commitment and perseverance of individual practitioners sustained by the focused efforts of the whole school community. Collaborative inquiry requires

*School improvement is not easy and quick. Data-driven change requires the commitment and perseverance of individual practitioners sustained by the focused efforts of the whole school community.*

the vulnerability to learn in public, be patient with process, and suspend self-interest to serve a larger purpose. Groups that embrace these challenges, invest energy in their own development, and put data in the center of their conversations produce significant learning gains for themselves and their students.

We invite you to use this book as one vehicle on your road to learning. To accelerate your progress, use the exercises in each chapter individually or as a group study. Exploring the web resources will open further avenues for investigation. While at times the road ahead might be steep or bumpy, we believe the journey will both exhilarate and surprise you.

# CHAPTER ONE

# Developing Cultures of Collaborative Inquiry

In a rapidly changing world, the role of teaching and teachers has remained highly stable. Images from novels, old photographs, and movies portray instructors at the front and center of the classroom, delivering lessons to sometimes docile, sometimes unruly groups of students. When the backstage life of teachers is depicted, we see staffrooms filled with banter, gossip, and complaint. In these settings, social interaction with other adults is a way station offering respite from the arduous work of enlightening young minds.

Outdated expectations and structures cannot meet the learning needs of today's students. Data bounce off these entrenched cultures of individualism, cultures that maintain isolated pockets of both excellence and mediocrity in the same organization with no mechanisms for sharing and transferring success (Newman, King, & Rigdon, 1997). A cohesive approach to school improvement requires new ways of thinking about and structuring teachers' work. The emerging models of professional engagement rally all resources to produce greater *cumulative* effects on student achievement.

Some teachers still perceive working with colleagues outside the classroom as shifting away from their real work with students. However, in this changing climate, collaborative interaction is, in fact, as much a part of teachers' work as is their time in the classroom with students.

> *Outdated expectations and structures cannot meet the learning needs of today's students. . . . A cohesive approach to school improvement requires new ways of thinking about and structuring teachers' work.*

## Shifting Values, Shifting Cultures

As work cultures evolve, the underlying values and beliefs inherent in shifting models are in transition. Table 1.1 (page 8) describes four major value shifts. Each value shift encompasses a set of related beliefs and observable behaviors that emerge from these beliefs.

### From Professional Autonomy to Collaborative Practice

In cultures of high professional autonomy, the dominant values are entitlement and individualism. A strong belief in privacy translates to closed classroom

**Table 1.1: Four Value Shifts**

| Shifting From | Shifting To |
|---|---|
| Professional autonomy | Collaborative practice |
| Knowledge delivery | Knowledge construction |
| Externally mandated improvement | Internally motivated improvement |
| Quick fix | Continuous growth |

doors, protection of turf, and a perspective that data reflect personal success or failure. These are cultures of *my*: my content—you can't tell me what and what not to teach; my book—you can't teach it; my unit—you can't alter it; my materials—you can't use them; and my students—you can't talk about them. In these cultures, the locus of change is the individual teacher. Teachers working in schools where this value is strong operate in isolation from one another, holding on to all of their personal strengths and weaknesses inside their private domains. Professional development becomes either a private choice or an imposed remediation.

In cultures of collaborative practice, the dominant value is co-construction of a shared knowledge base. The belief that teachers learn best with others drives the use of common assessments to inform individual and collective practice. Teachers share resources and strategies, successes and failures. They engage in systematic and ongoing experimentation and analyze data to learn from and with their students and colleagues.

In these cultures, the group is the focus of change, paying attention to its interactions and the cumulative effects being produced for students. Gap analysis and ongoing data exploration drive the professional learning agendas, not individual passion, interest, or the trend du jour. Professional development is a collective resource, not a personal prerogative. Peer engagement forges powerful links between teacher learning and student growth.

## *From Knowledge Delivery to Knowledge Construction*

In a knowledge delivery model, the classroom is the domain of the individual teacher, who controls the learning. In this authority culture, there are right and wrong answers, and students are expected to passively comply. Teachers uniformly dispense information aimed at covering the curriculum. Failure is seen as the student's fault; an intellectual or motivational deficit. In these classrooms, isolated learners sit row by row, competing with classmates for rank and reward. Summative data are used to demonstrate success or failure. Assessment is done *to* students. Teachers record and report grades, and instruction moves on.

In a knowledge construction model, the purpose of education is to create self-reliant learners. In this social learning climate, knowledge is co-constructed; students are critical thinkers and collaborators in learning. Teaching choices are in response to student needs. Teaching is for understanding and application of concepts and skills. Student grouping is flexible, based on skill level and interests, within each classroom and between classes. Colleagues invest in the success of all students. In this model, teachers use formative data to determine student growth and identify gaps to address. Students are full participants in the assessment process. Assessment is a tool for learning, and instructional decisions are based on learners' needs.

## From Externally Mandated Improvement to Internally Motivated Improvement

When improvement is externally mandated, state and provincial agents develop and use data management systems to peer inside schools and publicly judge success and failure. Technical experts analyze data, identify gaps, and deliver prescriptions for groups to implement. Those in authority determine success criteria, how and when professionals should talk, and what they should talk about. This forced interaction disguises and ritualizes collegiality, as individuals sit together in the same room at the same time working on assigned tasks.

In this environment, the pressure to be accountable creates coerced responses, not thoughtful action. Teachers do not control how and when to measure learning and which data to collect and report. Assessment is something that is done to, and not by, teachers.

> *Assessment is something that is done to, and not by, teachers.*

When improvement is internally driven, teachers are choice makers, owning both questions and answers. They are confident and skillful data users, motivated to continually increase their skillfulness, seeking multiple sources of data and methods for exploring them. Shared responsibility for student success is the organizing value.

In this environment, collegial interaction amplifies the drive to share and spread effective practice, creating new ways to work with students and one another. Collaborative teams explore data for patterns and the root causes for success and performance gaps. Teachers share ownership for taking both individual and collective responsibility for growth.

## From Quick Fix to Continuous Growth

In a quick-fix culture, short-term thinking and the need for immediate success dominate the conversation. This orientation results in short-cycle planning and implementation and intervention or remedial models. Improvement is about fixing what shows, going for visible, easily measurable results that don't require deep changes in practice. This approach to *gaming the system* (Hargreaves & Shirley, 2009) focuses on raising scores by targeting instruction to those students who hover at the margin of success.

In a continuous-growth culture, improving the fundamental depth and quality of teaching and learning organizes the conversation. This orientation requires complex, and often controversial, changes in instructional practice, subject identity, and school structures (Hargreaves & Shirley, 2009). Time horizons stretch beyond the school year for goals, plans, and measurements.

Teams use short-cycle assessments formatively to monitor progress and calibrate refinements in longer-term plans. These data focus and energize the collaborative conversation for continual improvement.

# Defining, Developing, and Sustaining High-Performing Cultures

Significant and stable changes in student performance require not only changes in classroom practices but also changes in the working culture of teachers. All cultural change requires leaders to recognize patterns and determine which patterns of interaction are productive and which patterns are not. All groups, both large and small, develop norms around the distribution and uses of influence, authority, and power (Schein, 2004). How these norms play out in a given group forms the baseline from which any changes will emerge. Developing and sustaining high-performing cultures is an ongoing learning process that requires pattern breaking of unproductive patterns and conscious pattern making of robust and constructive ways of working together.

Organizational cultures reflect written and unwritten rules that are based on underlying assumptions and values. These values are expressed in actions and artifacts: in the language, symbols, ceremonies, rituals, and reward systems; in approaches to problem solving; and in the design of the work environment (Deal & Peterson, 1999; Schein, 2004).

Within an organization, various subsets including grade-level teams, departments, and data teams also embody and express unique group personalities based on collective values and assumptions. Culture influences four key drivers of a group's work: (1) focus, or what captures the group's attention; (2) commitment, or the degree to which individuals identify with the group; (3) motivation, or the willingness to invest time and energy within meetings and outside of them; and (4) productivity, or the degree of goal achievement (Deal & Peterson, 1999). These cultural elements both inform and direct the ways in which a group sees itself, treats its members, and engages with its tasks. Ingrained behavioral patterns result from deep, unconscious drivers. When these invisible elements are brought to the surface and made visible, groups can shape and strengthen both their processes and their results.

# Describing the Seven Qualities of High-Performing Groups

A work culture is not static. Culture is both a noun and a verb, and is shaped by the continued shared experiences of the group and the processing of these experiences. The resulting adjustments in behaviors influence the beliefs and assumptions that ultimately become the new operating norms.

In schools, the quality of the adult culture directly affects the learning environment for students. The presence of a professional community that is centered on student learning makes a significant difference to measurable student achievement (Bolam, McMahon, Stoll, Thomas, & Wallace, 2005; Louis & Marks, 1998).

The power of this connection compels us to examine and define the interactions between adults that produce the most positive results for learners and learning. That is, what makes a group culture powerful, and what can we do to make it even more so?

The following seven actions describe high-performing groups.

1. Maintain a clear focus.
2. Embrace a spirit of inquiry.
3. Put data at the center.
4. Honor commitments to learners and learning.
5. Cultivate relational trust.
6. Seek equity.
7. Assume collective responsibility.

These qualities are lenses through which groups and individual group members can view their interactions to gain perspective on the choices that they are making and the skills they are applying as they work together.

Group development also requires personal development. When and how group members choose to participate emerges from individual and collective awareness and commitment to developing these attributes.

### Maintain a Clear Focus

High-performing groups clarify desired results and define success criteria. Less-productive groups meander from topic to topic, often within overcrowded agendas. Such groups use a scattershot approach in which all items are treated with equal importance. High-performing groups agree on and protect priorities for themselves and their students, preserving precious time for focused engagement about the things that matter.

By establishing clear and measurable goals and using success criteria to determine progress, these groups can work in the present while holding longer-term visions for improvement (Jaques & Cason, 1994). These groups are willing to sustain focus for extended periods of time. For example, achieving high levels of reading comprehension for all students requires significant attention and innovation in instructional and assessment practices. The results of these changes for large cohorts of students may not appear in the short term, but they will increase over time with ongoing monitoring and adjustments informed by data-driven conversations.

High-performing groups manage and minimize the constant distractions. Agreed-on structures and signals supply *digression management*, particularly when time is short, energy is low, and tasks are demanding. For example, such groups have prioritized and time-coded public agendas to guide time monitoring and shorthand language, such as *birdwalk alert*, when the conversation wanders away from the topic at hand.

In these groups, members self-monitor, paying attention to themselves and each other, to gauge whether their contributions add to or detract from the group's focus. There is an agreement that maintaining focus is more important than any individual's desire to share an anecdote or elaboration.

## Embrace a Spirit of Inquiry

High-performing groups ask genuine questions (Schwarz, 2002) about their own processes and practices, as well as their students' learning. They inquire. By definition, inquiry means you do not have a preferred response or do not already know the answer. As Goldberg (1998) states, "Because questions are intrinsically related to action, they spark and direct attention, perception, energy, and effort, and so are at the heart of the evolving forms that our lives assume" (p. 3). Less-productive groups avoid ambiguity, uncertainty, and challenging questions, wrapping themselves in and drawing on the comfort of their existing knowledge base.

High-performing groups are both problem seekers and problem solvers. These groups seek external resources and data outside their own experience. Such groups consider an *and/both* approach, not *right/wrong* or *either/or* responses, skillfully engaging in conflict with ideas, not with one another. They inquire into data to explore who is learning and who is not, seeking patterns and root causes before pursuing solutions and planning actions.

In these groups, members are willing to suspend their own judgments and opinions as they consider other perspectives. They are willing to delay solution generation. They push past surface ideas and avoid the comfort of quick conclusions, seeking external resources to extend their own knowledge base.

## Put Data at the Center

High-performing groups use data to inform and guide group and student learning. These data focus and calibrate conversations. Less-productive groups blur fact and opinion, occupying time with anecdote and argument. High-performing groups tap multiple types and multiple sources of data to move their work forward. For example, a group might examine student work products, standardized test scores, and classroom-based assessment to reveal a fuller picture of student performance in a specific skill area.

By exploring both formative and summative sources and using shared protocols and structures, these groups are able to depersonalize the data and use them as a catalyst for rich conversations about practice, learning, and progress toward desired goals. With skillful inquiry and balanced participation, they delve beneath the surface features of the data, persevering in the quest for deeper understandings.

*Less-productive groups blur fact and opinion, occupying time with anecdote and argument. High-performing groups tap multiple types and multiple sources of data to move their work forward.*

In these groups, members are assessment literate. They keep data central to the conversation, seeking out and using multiple sources and multiple types to inform their choices and plans. They make sure the data are available to, visible to, and understood by everyone.

## Honor Commitments to Learners and Learning

High-performing groups keep learning as the focus of their conversations. They see themselves and all members as learners, and they are willing to consider the limits of their own knowledge. This essential disposition energizes the learning potential within the group and extends to high-powered learning for students. Less-productive groups stay within the boundaries of their current capabilities and are satisfied with merely meeting expectations, not exceeding them, both for themselves and for their students.

High-performing groups keep their focus on what is good for students, not just convenient for themselves. They explore the process, performance, and products of learning. They also assess and monitor their own learning, reflecting on their processes and products and setting goals for continuous improvement.

In these groups, members explore learning for all students, not just select groups. They seek to improve learning for the high performers, as well as those who may be struggling. As committed learners themselves, they understand that their students' growth links to their own.

## Cultivate Relational Trust

High-performing groups operate with high expectations and positive intentions as central assumptions. Within these groups, it is safe to display both high competence and vulnerability. In less-productive groups, members fear attack or reprisal for things they might do or say, and they are filled with doubt, having little or no faith that their colleagues will honor decisions or follow through on agreements. High-performing groups rely on the integrity and competence of their colleagues inside and outside of the meeting room. When it is safe not to know, teachers seek the counsel of their peers; they don't feel the need to hide their shortcomings (McLaughlin & Talbert, 2001). They can count on fellow group members' reliable and consistent application of team agreements to their own professional practice.

In these groups, members say what they'll do and do what they said. They assume positive intentionality and believe in the goodwill of their colleagues. They understand the difference between a question and a critique. For this reason, they are willing to be vulnerable and disclose both their successes and shortcomings, knowing that this information will not be exploited or belittled. They hold high expectations for themselves and each other and have faith that those expectations will be met and even exceeded.

## Seek Equity

High-performing groups leave titles, seniority, and role authority at the door. On this level playing field, they seek a diverse blend of voices and protect space for all to contribute. Less-productive groups limit participation and restrict divergent thought, sealing themselves in the protection of their own logic. They congratulate themselves for small successes and rationalize performance gaps.

High-performing groups ensure reciprocity, foster interdependence, and engage in productive collaboration. They apply structures to ensure that the data shy and the data literate have equal voice in the conversation as all strive for shared understanding. For example, such groups provide equal opportunities to join the conversations by creating smaller task groups that focus on large, shared data displays; using round-robin protocols to balance participation; and publicly charting so ideas belong to everyone.

In these groups, members operate from the assumption that everyone has something to offer. They monitor their own level of participation to be sure they are not dominating the conversation and make sure to encourage participation, especially from those who have not yet shared.

## Assume Collective Responsibility

High-performing groups make and honor agreements about who they want to be as a group and what they want to produce for their students. They make data-driven choices and are willing to be answerable for those choices. This collective efficacy, or the shared belief that together the group will successfully achieve its goals, is a prime resource for sustained improvements in student learning (Goddard, Hoy, & Woolfolk Hoy, 2004). In less-productive groups, members are protective of their autonomy in the meeting room and in the classroom. They are unwilling to see others' work as part of their own. They don't believe that team members have the capability and willingness to make a difference.

Groups with high degrees of collective responsibility pursue challenging goals, exert concentrated effort, and persist in collective action leading to improved performance for the group and their students (Goddard, Hoy, & Woolfolk Hoy, 2000). In these groups, members believe in the power of the group to make a difference for students. They recognize that their individual choices, both in the meeting room and in their classrooms, affect everyone.

Thus, they willingly invest their time and energy, setting aside personal agendas to support the group's work and its development.

# Drawing on Feedback

High-performing groups draw on internal and external sources, or feedback, to monitor and modify their performance. Feedback is information to the system. Developing groups use multiple types of feedback to modify, control, or change their products and performance. In the absence of feedback, groups stagnate. Valuing and applying the insights that emerge from well-constructed feedback is both an essential disposition and a learned skill for thoughtful group members and thoughtful groups.

Effective feedback both maintains and amplifies high performance. Maintaining feedback reinforces established parameters, such as learning standards. Amplifying feedback increases desired behaviors so that they spread throughout the system. For example, skillful groups use student performance data to determine whether and which students are meeting established standards, so they can continue to achieve these same results. They might then use the same data to determine where and how to transfer effective practices to increase success in other areas and for other students.

To assess, maintain, and amplify the seven qualities, a group requires specific feedback mechanisms. The following tables are two such instruments. Table 1.2 provides group questions to measure and maintain a group's present feedback practices. Table 1.3 (page 16) provides self-assessment questions that stimulate deep reflection about personal choices and behaviors to amplify feedback. The essential questions in each table will help groups and group members understand who they are in light of who they want to be. (See pages 21–23 for reproducible versions of these tables.)

**Table 1.2: Seven Qualities of High-Performing Groups—Scaled Group Inventory**

| Quality | Questions for Groups | Scale: 1–4 (Rarely to Always) |
|---|---|---|
| **Maintain a clear focus.** | Are we clear about our desired results in both the short and long term? | |
| | Do we have clear and shared criteria for determining success? | |
| | Do we have strategies for getting back on track if focus is lost? | |
| **Embrace a spirit of inquiry.** | Do we ask questions for which we have no immediate answers? | |
| | Do we search for and honor other perspectives? | |
| | Are we willing to ask questions that might cause discomfort? | |

continued→

| Quality | Questions for Groups | Scale: 1–4 (Rarely to Always) |
|---|---|---|
| Put data at the center. | Do we use data to calibrate and inform our conversations? | |
| | Do we use multiple types and sources of data to add to our thinking? | |
| | Do we have methods for ensuring shared understanding? | |
| Honor commitments to learners and learning. | Are our conversations student centered? | |
| | Do we continually assess our current learning goals (for students and for ourselves as a group)? | |
| | Do we set meaningful goals for our own learning as a group? | |
| Cultivate relational trust. | Do we clarify and communicate high expectations for ourselves as a group? | |
| | Do we make it safe not to know? | |
| | Do our actions reflect our commitments? | |
| Seek equity. | Do we use structures and protocols to ensure balanced participation? | |
| | Do all group members have an equal voice? | |
| | Do we challenge our own preferences and judgments in order to consider other ideas? | |
| Assume collective responsibility. | Do we believe that our collective action makes a greater difference for student learning than our individual efforts? | |
| | Are we willing to be answerable for the choices we are making? | |
| | Do we push past *good enough* to continually challenge ourselves? | |

Table 1.3: Seven Qualities of High-Performing Groups—Self-Assessment Inventory

| Quality | Questions for Individual Group Members | Comments |
|---|---|---|
| Maintain a clear focus. | Am I clear about our purpose? | |
| | Is this comment or contribution contributing to our purpose? (Do I really need to say this?) | |
| | Should I refocus the group at this point? | |
| Embrace a spirit of inquiry. | Am I asking questions to which I have an answer? | |
| | Am I open to the influence of others' perspectives? | |
| | What might I be avoiding or leaving out? | |

| Quality | Questions for Individual Group Members | Comments |
|---|---|---|
| **Put data at the center.** | How do these data influence my thinking and comments? | |
| | What other sources might add to our thinking? | |
| | What don't I understand at this point? | |
| **Honor commitments to learners and learning.** | How do I keep learning as the priority? | |
| | In what ways am I achieving my current goals in my classroom and with my group? | |
| | What new goals might I set for my own learning? | |
| **Cultivate relational trust.** | What makes me feel safe or not in this group? | |
| | How am I making it safe for others? | |
| | Am I following through on my commitments? | |
| **Seek equity.** | Am I talking too much? Too little? | |
| | Do others have space to share? | |
| | Am I able to set my own preferences and judgments aside to consider others' ideas? | |
| **Assume collective responsibility.** | How am I demonstrating my investment in this group? | |
| | How is my participation affecting others in the group? | |
| | In what ways are the connections and linkages between my work and my colleagues' work making a difference for students? | |

For most groups, there is a tension between investing time in capacity building and completing the immediate task; many complete the immediate task at the expense of capacity building. Yet when groups only focus on their work, their skill and resource levels remain static. High-performing groups recognize that meeting the complex challenges and commitment to ongoing improvement of student learning requires equal commitment to their own growth.

• • • • • • • **Data Story: Committing to Group Growth** • • • • • • •

It is midyear at Prairie View Elementary School. The fourth-grade team has a weekly forty-five-minute work session and has been working together for two years. This year, two new teachers have joined the six-member group. The group members have targeted math as an area for improvement. While all agree that their work has been productive, they want to continue to develop as a high-performing group. Using the Scaled Group Inventory (page 21) as a basis for dialogue, the team members have established goals for their own growth as they explore math data.

Based on their conversation, they have selected two qualities: (1) maintaining a clear focus and (2) developing relational trust, as their goal arenas for the year.

At this point in their development, they have agreed to focus on effectively using time (digression management) and ensuring a sense of emotional safety for all members as key growth areas.

To assess time use, they have agreed to create a rotating role of *process observer*. This group member, while engaging in the task at hand, will keep a record of both on- and off-task or topic time use. They will use these data comparatively from meeting to meeting to determine their increasing efficiency.

Keeping data at the center, they will also use an exit survey format at the end of each meeting. Each team member will respond to two stems to assess growth in relational trust.

    *1. Something that made me feel safe during this meeting is _____.*

    *2. Something I did to make others feel safe is _____.*

The team members preserve twenty minutes of processing time every other meeting to discuss their own growth.

    "Look at the graph for our on- or off-task time use. On-task time is increasing, but not very rapidly."

    "Yes, I expected by this time of year we would have at least 90 percent of our time on task, but it's only 65 percent."

    "Maybe 90 percent isn't realistic, given that we do need some decompression conversation and to connect about stuff that happens between meetings."

    "Well, let's say we aim for 80 percent, what can we do to meet that target?"

    "How about using a visible timer, a signal when we meander off topic, or both?"

    "And let's reserve five minutes at the beginning of each meeting for some social interaction, catching up and touching base—then get down to business."

    "So, for our next meeting, let's have a little bell in the middle of the table that anyone can access if the conversation strays away from the topic and see how that works."

    "Yes, and let's have a coffee and conversation space at the beginning of our session—but let's be sure to keep it to five minutes."

    "Maybe that's where the public timer could come in, as well!"

Once the group has agreed to some action related to its time-use goal, the members explore their data on relational trust. They put the exit slips from the last two meetings on the table and sort them into categories.

    "It seems that there are some consistent examples of things that increase our emotional safety, like not being interrupted or feeling like we have a space to speak, which come up in more than half of the responses; not interrupting others appears frequently as well."

"That's great—but what are we not seeing that would be important to be there?"

"Well, it would be important to feel like it's OK to not understand the data or even some of the math content and to be able to say so."

"Let's talk about how we might ensure that degree of safety."

This dialogue goes on for another few minutes, allowing all members to air their concerns and express their satisfactions.

• • • • • • • • • • • • • • • • • • • • • • • • • • • • • • • • • • • • • • • •

# Exercise Your Learning

Complete the Scaled Group Inventory (page 21) to assess how the seven qualities of high-performing groups apply to a group with whom you are presently working. Use the results to structure a data-driven dialogue and to set goals for continued learning. To focus the interaction, make a public display on which to record responses.

Consider the following options for application.

- Ask individual group members to complete the inventory and compare responses as a group.

- Subdivide the group into pairs or trios to complete the inventory.

- Complete the inventory as a full group with public recording.

Note: In each case, be sure to generate specific examples to support the scaled responses.

Complete the Self-Assessment Inventory (page 22) as a reflection of your contributions to the seven qualities of high-performing groups. Use the results to structure a dialogue and to set personal goals for continued learning. Consider the following options for application.

- Ask individual group members to complete the inventory and compare responses as a group.

- Subdivide the group into pairs or trios for interaction about their results.

- Organize a group dialogue about relationships between individual reflections and the group's performance.

Visit **go.solution-tree.com/teams** to download the reproducibles and access the links in this book.

# Extend Your Learning

Meredith Belbin studies team roles, responsibilities, and interpersonal styles. The Mind Tools website has a useful tool for analyzing your team's roles based on Belbin's strategies (www.mindtools.com/pages/article/newLDR_83.htm; Mind Tools, n.d.a).

"Group Development Tools Practitioners Can Use" (Minahan & Hutton, 2002) is a practical article that lays out a basic model about groups and their behaviors (www.ntl.org/upload/GroupDevelopmentTools.pdf).

# Scaled Group Inventory

| Quality | Questions for Groups | Scale: 1–4 (Rarely to Always) |
|---|---|---|
| Maintain a clear focus. | Are we clear about our desired results in both the short and long term? | |
| | Do we have clear and shared criteria for determining success? | |
| | Do we have strategies for getting back on track if focus is lost? | |
| Embrace a spirit of inquiry. | Do we ask questions for which we have no immediate answers? | |
| | Do we search for and honor other perspectives? | |
| | Are we willing to ask questions that might cause discomfort? | |
| Put data at the center. | Do we use data to calibrate and inform our conversations? | |
| | Do we use multiple types and sources of data to add to our thinking? | |
| | Do we have methods for ensuring shared understanding? | |
| Honor commitments to learners and learning. | Are our conversations student centered? | |
| | Do we continually assess our current learning goals (for students and for ourselves as a group)? | |
| | Do we set meaningful goals for our own learning as a group? | |
| Cultivate relational trust. | Do we clarify and communicate high expectations for ourselves as a group? | |
| | Do we make it safe not to know? | |
| | Do our actions reflect our commitments? | |
| Seek equity. | Do we use structures and protocols to ensure balanced participation? | |
| | Do all group members have an equal voice? | |
| | Do we challenge our own preferences and judgments in order to consider other ideas? | |
| Assume collective responsibility. | Do we believe that our collective action makes a greater difference for student learning than our individual efforts? | |
| | Are we willing to be answerable for the choices we are making? | |
| | Do we push past *good enough* to continually challenge ourselves? | |

# Self-Assessment Inventory

## Maintain a Clear Focus

1. Am I clear about our purpose? _____

_____

2. Is this comment or contribution contributing to our purpose? (Do I really need to say this?) _____

_____

3. Should I refocus the group at this point? _____

_____

## Embrace a Spirit of Inquiry

1. Am I asking questions to which I have an answer? _____

_____

2. Am I open to the influence of others' perspectives? _____

_____

3. What might I be avoiding or leaving out? _____

_____

## Put Data at the Center

1. How do these data influence my thinking and comments? _____

_____

2. What other sources might add to our thinking? _____

_____

3. What don't I understand at this point? _____

_____

## Honor Commitments to Learners and Learning

1. How do I keep learning as the priority? _____

_____

page 1 of 2

2. In what ways am I achieving my current goals in my classroom and with my group? _____

_____

3. What new goals might I set for my own learning? _____

_____

## Cultivate Relational Trust

1. What makes me feel safe or not in this group? _____

_____

2. How am I making it safe for others? _____

_____

3. Am I following through on my commitments? _____

_____

## Seek Equity

1. Am I talking too much? Too little? _____

_____

2. Do others have space to share? _____

_____

3. Am I able to set my own preferences and judgments aside to consider others' ideas? _____

_____

## Assume Collective Responsibility

1. How am I demonstrating my investment in this group? _____

_____

2. How is my participation affecting others in the group? _____

_____

3. In what ways are the connections and linkages between my work and my colleagues' work making a difference for students? _____

_____

# CHAPTER TWO

# *Introducing the Collaborative Learning Cycle*

Productive conversations require shape and structure. Thoughtfully designed processes increase focus, minimize distractions, and deepen exploration and analysis of data. Without such processes, group work disintegrates into excessive storytelling, over-certain and over-sold solutions, and a premature rush to action spearheaded by just a few members of the group.

Consistently applied frameworks develop shared expertise and confidence with collaborative data work. These satisfying and productive experiences have a cumulative effect, creating positive expectations for the productive use of time and achievement of relevant outcomes. The *collaborative learning cycle* (Wellman & Lipton, 2004) we describe here is a field-tested model for achieving to these aims.

The collaborative learning cycle is a framework that establishes a learning forum for group exploration of data (see figure 2.1, page 26). Structured engagement with information and fellow learners ignites the processes of inquiry and problem solving. This question-driven model promotes specific cognitive processes and group-member interaction in three phases: (1) activating and engaging, (2) exploring and discovering, and (3) organizing and integrating.

The first phase—activating and engaging—develops emotional and cognitive readiness for collaborative work with data. The second phase—exploring and discovering—invites thoughtful observations from multiple perspectives, producing a deep look at the data. The third phase—organizing and integrating—has two distinct stages. Initially, the group selects key observations and generates possible causes for those results. After clarifying theories with additional data, the group then generates potential action plans.

> *Structured engagement with information and fellow learners ignites the processes of inquiry and problem solving.*

**Activating and Engaging**

*Surfacing experiences and expectations*

What assumptions do we bring to this discussion?

What questions are we asking?

What are some possibilities for learning that this experience presents to us?

**Organizing and Integrating**

*Generating theory*

What inferences, explanations, or conclusions might we draw? (causation)

What additional data sources might we explore to verify our explanation? (confirmation)

What solutions might we explore as a result of our conclusions? (action)

What data will we need to collect to guide implementation? (calibration)

Managing
Modeling
Mediating
Monitoring

**Exploring and Discovering**

*Analyzing the data*

What important points seem to pop out?

What patterns, categories, or trends are emerging?

What seems to be surprising or unexpected?

What are some ways we have not yet explored these data?

*Source: Wellman & Lipton, 2004.*

**Figure 2.1: The collaborative learning cycle—structuring dialogue for connection making.**

# Activating and Engaging: Surfacing Experiences and Expectations

Powerful, data-based explorations start by cultivating conscious curiosity rather than concern. This first phase establishes group work norms and shapes expectations for how the data exploration will occur. This is true for working with all types of data: quantitative or qualitative; formative or summative; local, state, provincial, or national.

## *Purpose*

Focusing attention for collaborative work is an ongoing challenge for busy educators. Readiness to explore data requires the full physical, cognitive, and emotional energy of all group members. The *activating and engaging phase* prepares group members for this work by eliciting assumptions about learners and learning, as those assumptions relate to the data the group is about to explore.

## Process

Groups begin with predictions prior to seeing any data and discuss what they anticipate the data might look like. These predictions illuminate areas of expectation and create anticipation and curiosity. For example, a group preparing to look at a math assessment might first start with blank copies of the graphs that it will later be examining. During the predicting phase, members would sketch in the bars or lines of the various performance bands as they envision the actual displays. Simultaneously, members would explore and record the assumptions on which those predictions are based. In this conversation, a group member might say, "Given this point in the year, I think that about 30 percent of the students will have advanced skills in the geometry portion of the assessment, and maybe another 20 to 25 percent will be at the mastery level. The rest will fall below expectations. We have a wide age range in the fifth grade this year, and my assumption is that the geometry concepts being tested are pretty abstract, and many of the younger students don't have the higher levels of cognitive maturity needed to understand and apply them."

By articulating their assumptions and predictions, individuals surface their frames of reference. For group members, this interaction increases understanding of the mental models that are guiding instructional decisions and teaching practices—their own and their colleagues'. It also establishes a foundation for viewing the data in the next phase, with an advance organizer that includes the features of the math assessment that produced the data. The scene is now set for detailed exploration of the data set. Distinguishing between assumptions and predictions is essential for developing shared understandings and seeing new possibilities. Opening up the assumption about cognitive maturity motivates a productive dialogue about math standards—the fit between curriculum and instructional approaches as they apply to this group of students and the technical details of the assessment.

The intentions of this phase are to surface perspectives and create readiness for looking at data. In some circumstances, the group has already seen the data or members are working with formative assessments, such as student work products or teacher checklists. In these cases, a provocative question or stem completion will create the appropriate emotional and cognitive preparation. For example, "What are some factors that contribute to student success in math, language arts, and so on?," "Successful teachers of writing, reading, science, and so on pay attention to _____," or "To be an effective data team, it's important that we _____."

## Potential

Perhaps most importantly, a well-crafted activating and engaging phase establishes psychological safety and emotional readiness for interacting with colleagues and the data. It is here that group members learn about themselves and their colleagues, learn that it is OK not to be sure initially, and learn that they will have a voice and a value in the group. Rather than engaging in a game of right and wrong, they learn what to expect from the data and each other, eliminating defensive postures and the need to attack or deny the information displayed before them.

By activating and engaging, groups surface and articulate existing knowledge about their own students and the learning processes that relate to the data about to be explored. This process also surfaces assumptions about beliefs and practices underpinning teaching and learning that are deeper than the immediate task. This purposeful engagement increases involvement and the perception of relevancy for the task, the data, and the group work.

## Pitfalls

The result of skipping this phase—for lack of time or lack of understanding its importance—is often misinterpretation and wide discrepancies in individual perceptions about the data being examined. Important voices get lost in a swirl of story and opinion. Volume is mistaken for persuasion. Without this preparation, there may be confusion when data are introduced during the exploring and discovering phase. Group members may enter with defensive postures or may be surprised, or even shocked, by the perspectives or observations that emerge.

> *Important voices get lost in a swirl of story and opinion. Volume is mistaken for persuasion.*

## Tips for Success

Carefully separating predictions from assumptions is an essential part of the activating and engaging phase. Applying these tips will increase your group's success.

- **Distinguish between predictions and assumptions:** Predictions are experience-based conjectures regarding what group members expect might appear in the data. Both predictions and assumptions arise from individuals' worldviews, which their knowledge, beliefs, and values inform. What distinguishes predictions from assumptions is that predictions will be visible in the data. For example, "I predict that on this benchmark writing assessment, the kids will score well on transition words, because I'm assuming that we all work consistently on that vocabulary starting in grade 3."

  Assumptions usually remain tacit and unquestioned. One important benefit of this phase is surfacing and examining individual and collective beliefs about learners and learning. A statement of experience such as "I've done this for fifteen years, and I always see this pattern" is not an assumption. In this circumstance, it is useful to inquire more deeply: "What are some of your assumptions about the consistency of this pattern?"

  As groups develop, group members become more skillful in clarifying the distinctions between predictions and assumptions. People don't always lead with, or label, one or the other. Oftentimes predictions and assumptions are blurred within one long statement. It is important to listen and sort, paraphrase and inquire. For example, you might hear, "I think there is going to be a wide gender discrepancy in the results for writing. Girls just read more than boys, and it's going to be reflected in their scores." To which you might respond, "So, you assume that reading and writing are highly correlated and that girls read more than boys? What are you predicting the differences might be, and what might the results look like within the various writing strands?"

- **Develop predictions, and surface related assumptions concurrently:** When a group member offers a prediction, the same person should also be encouraged to share the underlying assumption. When a group member shares an assumption, the same person should then generate a concrete prediction for how that assumption might appear in the data.

- **Record predictions and related assumptions:** Use separate recording sheets or charts for this purpose. The physical recording of predictions grounds the conversation, increases task focus, and builds shared understanding.

- **Record predictions on a facsimile of the data display:** When possible, use a graph or chart that reflects the actual format of the data display. This recording sheet serves as an advanced organizer for viewing the data at the next phase. This practice boosts confidence and readiness, saving time that might be needed for orienting to the actual display format.

- **Accept different predictions or assumptions:** The key function of dialogue at this stage is to seek to understand, not to persuade. Group work becomes bogged down when members struggle unnecessarily for consensus or engage in an assumptions debate. If necessary to move the dialogue forward, create and record more than one set of predictions and their related assumptions.

# Exploring and Discovering: Analyzing the Data

Analyzing data skillfully requires thoughtful process, emotional control, and mental focus. Working with data should be a learning experience. To maintain that intent, it is important to pay attention to careful structuring of the exploring and discovering phase.

## *Purpose*

Purposeful uncertainty is the guiding mindset of the exploring and discovering phase. This second phase is the heart of collaborative inquiry. To embrace a spirit of exploration and discovery, groups must avoid jumping to premature conclusion and closure. The late Bob Gore, former CEO of W. L. Gore and Associates, best known as the manufacturers of such innovative products as GORE-TEX® fabrics and Elixir® guitar strings, was renowned among his colleagues for his ability to ask insightful questions that reframed thinking. They referred to his systematic avoidance to rush to closure as *intellectual hang time*, likening this search for fresh perspectives and approaches to problems to the hang time of gifted basketball players, who seem to suspend themselves in the air as they search for an opening to the basket (Pacanowsky, 1995).

In a similar way, to remain open to possibilities and fresh viewpoints, groups must stay with the data and push to explore multiple storylines. This is the phase of distinguishing, sorting, analyzing, comparing, and contrasting.

## Process

No matter the group's size, exploring and discovering require data teams of four or five members, with each team working with shared, visually vibrant data displays. (See chapter 4, page 65, for more information on displays.) Larger working groups and too much data at one time lead to overload and disengagement.

*Data enthusiasts need to act as resources and refrain from dominating their groups and interpreting the data for them. The data shy need the confidence to ask what they fear might be obvious questions about the data or the displays.*

During this phase, both the data enthusiasts and the data shy have their own challenges. For inclusive, collaborative inquiry, the data enthusiasts need to act as resources and refrain from dominating their groups and interpreting the data for them. The data shy need the confidence to ask what they fear might be obvious questions about the data or the displays.

The data shy also need to be encouraged to share their ideas regarding what the data reflect about student performance. Individual observations are publicly charted, so they belong to the whole data team. For example, with a math group, a participant might observe, "Hey, here's a surprise given our initial assumption. If we sort the geometry strand results by birth date, there is very low correlation between the students' ages and their performance. See, this top-performing kid is one of the youngest in the class, and one of the low performers is the oldest."

In a similar way, skilled groups suspend certainty and continue to mine the data for a variety of observations and expressions of these observations.

## Potential

An effective exploring and discovering phase provides a shared focus for engagement and a systematic, balanced exploration of the data. In a well-structured experience, a group can mine the data more deeply and broadly than anyone working alone. This deep look helps group members see the data through others' eyes, especially those who have different perspectives, experiences, or specialized knowledge. This process often surfaces surprising observations or observations expressed in surprising ways.

During this phase, groups develop mutual understandings based on explicit expressions of the data, producing greater engagement, clarity, and perseverance. This phase actively reinforces the importance of collaborative exploration and opens the door to a wider view of the factors that might be producing the results at hand.

## Pitfalls

The most dangerous word to hear in this phase of collaborative inquiry is *because*. Once group members start explaining *why* the data look as they do, they often stop exploring and lock into biased descriptions and cursory explanations for both high and low performance. That is, once groups start analyzing, they stop observing and can miss observations or crucial details. Once explanations begin, the voices of those who seem confident, or who have social or role authority, often prevail. Groups may overlook vital possibilities and move to the next phase without shared understanding. Deviation from the intention of this phase cuts off exploration and often results in ill-defined problems and premature solutions.

## Tips for Success

Thoughtful attention to process design is a key factor in increasing focus and productive interaction in this phase. Applying these tips will increase your group's success.

- **Purposefully structure the workspace:** Create a shared focus for each data team by placing chairs in a semicircle around a central data display. This arrangement provides equal access to the data and keeps all group members examining the same data points at the same time. Without this common focal point, groups disintegrate into isolated individuals or subsets.

- **Provide time to orient to the data displays before talking:** Two to three minutes of silence equalizes opportunity for each group member to prepare for exploring the data. This pause honors the different pacing and processing needs of individuals and produces more balanced engagement.

- **Develop a sequence for exploration, and designate a starting point:** When multiple data sets or complex displays are on view, agreement on initial talking points saves time and energy and maximizes momentum and focus.

- **Apply structures and protocols to balance participation:** Deliberately structuring group work increases engagement, focus, and time efficiency. For example, assigning roles (such as recorder, process checker, materials manager, and timekeeper) or providing individual thinking and writing time before talking ensures each group member access to information and an opportunity to contribute. (See Group Work Structures, page 92.)

- **Establish a public recording protocol:** Create common charts or recording space for observations. Keep a separate chart for questions or comments that are outside the phase. For example, should conclusions or explanations surface, it is sometimes expedient to record them rather than debate them. This process is also effective for questions that are not directly relevant to the data.

- **Chart observations in language that is concise and specific:** Each observation statement should communicate a single idea clearly and concisely. These statements should focus only on observable facts contained in the data without interpretation or inference. Relevant data terminology, such as mean, median, mode, range, and distribution, increases the precision of the observation. (See table 2.1 for sample observations.)

- **Depersonalize the data:** Enlarged data displays, accompanied by specific physical and verbal patterns, depersonalize the data. These displays represent the third point for a collaborative conversation and help focus full attention. Three-point communication (Grinder, 1997) creates a triangle with the facilitator as one point, the group as a second point, and the data as the third point. This structure helps group members focus on the data rather than on each other, thereby reducing defensiveness, increasing resourcefulness, eliminating certainty postures, and developing shared ownership. These patterns give group members greater permission to talk about the data and name gaps, with less sense of finger-pointing. Using neutral language, such as *these data* or *this chart* rather than *your students* or *our performance results*, objectifies the data, making them easier to talk about.

**Table 2.1: From Rough to Refined Observations**

| Rough Observations | Refined Observations |
|---|---|
| There are more English learners (ELs) this year. | The EL population increased from 10 percent last year to 30 percent this year. |
| There is a downward performance trend from grade 5 to grade 7. | Thirty-eight percent of fifth graders were proficient compared to 12 percent of seventh graders. |
| Almost half of grade 10 students are below the standard in literacy. | Nineteen percent of grade 10 students performed at the below basic level, and 29 percent performed at the basic level in literacy. |
| There is a real spread in the score for third-grade girls in math. | The median score for third-grade girls is 45 percent at or above standard. |
| Most of the students didn't punctuate correctly on this writing sample. | Fourteen of the twenty students didn't capitalize accurately on this writing sample. |

*Source: Lipton & Wellman, 2010.*

# Organizing and Integrating: Generating Theory

Moving from analysis to understanding and then to action requires skillful process facilitation of the organizing and integrating phase.

## *Purpose*

The third phase of the collaborative learning cycle—organizing and integrating—establishes the transition to formal problem finding and problem solving as it builds a foundation for detailed planning processes. This phase occurs in two stages, *causation* and *action*. Groups need to stay open to multiple interpretations of why the data look as they do before developing any plans of action. Most data sets do not tell the whole story. For any explanation of causal factors to be credible, the analysis must be thoughtful and based on multiple, rich sources of information. Therefore, this phase includes collecting and reviewing additional data indicated by the theories of causation that emerge. Confirmation builds confidence in and commitment to the ultimate implementation plan. Multiple voices and multiple perspectives serve the work in each stage of organizing and integrating.

## *Process*

During this phase, groups first generate potential theories of causation related to key observations they made in the previous phase and then propose theories of action. That is, groups ask, "Why did we get these results? What caused these outcomes?"

### Stage One: Causation

Theories of causation tend to fall into one of five categories: (1) curriculum, (2) instruction, (3) teachers, (4) students, or (5) infrastructure. (See figure 2.2, page 34.) In the math data discussion illustrated in the activating and engaging phase, several theories might emerge. For example, "I think we are getting these results because the current instructional materials don't scaffold the fundamental geometric concepts for our more concrete learners" (causal category: instruction—materials). Or, "The unit on geometry is taught late in the spring, and there's little time to teach fully or to reinforce concepts for students who need reinforcement, or who might not have gotten them" (causal category: infrastructure—schedules).

Often, an individual's theory of causation is based on his or her own experience. For example, staff developers tend to suggest teacher knowledge and skill as an issue and more workshops as the solution. Curriculum experts suggest it's a lack of fidelity to the curricular objectives that causes low results. By extending the dialogue, surfacing a variety of causal theories, and confirming them with additional data, the deeper sources or root causes of the problem emerge.

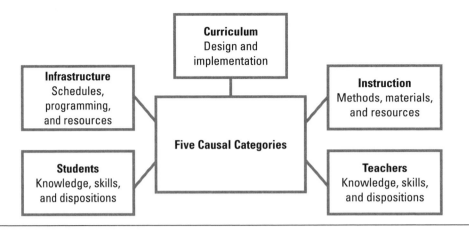

**Figure 2.2: Five causal categories.**

Confidence in any selected theory of causation increases when additional data sources confirm and elaborate the nuances of that theory. Subgroups of teachers then generate multiple causal theories and collect and explore related data before reporting back their findings to the larger committee working on this issue. By carefully considering these additional data sources, groups can then refine their theory or theories of causation and start to consider theories of action. For example, a fourth-grade team working with an expository writing assessment indicating low student performance might decide on several causal theories to explore: (1) the writing instruction is not appropriately balanced between narrative and expository writing instruction, (2) the reading instruction is not appropriately balanced between fiction and nonfiction forms, (3) the specific skill of vocabulary and word choice is an area of concern, and (4) teachers lack instructional repertoire for teaching expository writing. A subset of teachers from the team could then seek further data to clarify or confirm each of these theories to refine and enrich the theory of causation that will drive the team's action planning. (See chapter 3, page 43, for additional information on root-cause analysis.)

### Stage Two: Action

Once an exploration of multiple data sources confirms a potential cause, the team develops an action plan to address that cause. For example, "Now that we're pretty sure that it's an instructional issue, let's develop some outcomes for improving learning in geometry. We'll need to clarify the essential understandings for this math strand and then develop instructional scaffolds for building conceptual foundations for all of our students."

Effective plans include clear outcomes, measureable criteria for success, the necessary action steps, and a data-driven monitoring system for determining short- and long-term goal achievement. (See chapter 7, page 113, for more information on action planning.)

## Potential

Effectively implementing this phase builds ownership of problems and shared commitment to actions. It
increases motivation for change in practice and program.
This collective responsibility for student learning is a
hallmark of improving schools (Hoy, Tarter, & Woolfolk-
Hoy, 2006).

## Pitfalls

*Effective plans include
clear outcomes, measureable
criteria for success, the
necessary action steps, and
a data-driven monitoring
system for determining
short- and long-term
goal achievement.*

The tendency toward rapid closure on a single theory
of action causes problems in this phase. Groups pressed by time and a sense of
urgency often prefer any action to further reflection. Their desire to serve the
immediate learning needs of students often derails deeper explorations, and
they then overlook the embedded patterns that may be producing the very
learning gaps being addressed or the learning successes that might be amplified.

## Tips for Success

The organizing and integrating phase is complex and shifts modes of discourse from dialogue to discussion to decision. Going slow at this point is ultimately a way of accelerating the improvement process.

- **Study success:** Select an observation from the previous phase that reflects successful performance, such as an improvement trend, a high-
  level skill that stands out on a rubric or benchmark assessment, or a spike
  on a bar graph for a particular group of students. Develop causal theories
  for what might have produced that success.

- **Generate multiple theories of causation:** One important outcome of
  the causation stage is to consider multiple possibilities before locking
  in on a limited explanation. Stretch the group's thinking by using the
  five causal categories to generate diverse explanations for observable
  results. Groups should intentionally develop theories in more than one
  category.

- **Allow for multiple causal theories:** When group members seem to be
  invested in different theories, reduce potential polarization by calibrating data for more than one causal theory. Subdivide this task based on
  interest, passion, or technical knowledge.

- **Seek calibrating data that are in existing archives:** Given time and energy constraints, it is useful to look first to archival data to confirm, correct,
  or clarify causal theories. Archival data include student performance results, such as test scores, grades, and attendance records; demographic
  data, such as percent of English learners or special education students in
  a grade level; and staff statistics, such as education or experience levels.
  (See chapter 4, page 64, for more information on archival data.)

- **Generate multiple theories of solution:** There are no simple answers for complex problems. Successful improvement plans require multiple intervention points and interrelated approaches. At this stage in the data cycle, groups should push for a wide range of possible pathways for promoting growth.

- **Make sure goals are clear and measureable:** It is useful to provide guidelines and criteria for goal setting to ensure that everyone understands and is ready to engage in a shared pursuit of excellence. One effective model is based on SMART goals (O'Neill & Conzemius, 2006). SMART goals are specific and strategic, measureable, attainable, results oriented, and time bound. (See chapter 7, page 115, for more information on planning and SMART goals.)

Groups that take the time to develop and engage in cycles of data-driven inquiry create more enduring solutions and greater commitment to those solutions. When they employ structural scaffolds such as the collaborative learning cycle, they experience increased confidence, perseverance, and success in working productively with data and with each other. By using data to tell our stories to one another, we create new possibilities for professional practice and new possibilities for the students we serve.

• • • • **Data Story: Working With Formative Writing Data** • • • •

It is autumn in New England. Based on a three-year trend in state writing assessments, Ralph Waldo Emerson Middle School has targeted improvement in expository writing for this school year. The six teachers on the language arts team are gathered for their weekly meeting. Their task is to examine the first common assessment results for eighth-grade writing. The students produced a constructed response to the prompt "Was Mrs. Mitty a nagging wife?" The teachers chuckle, remembering that the source of this assignment was a debate that erupted in Mrs. Simon's class during a discussion of the classic James Thurber (1939) story, *The Secret Life of Walter Mitty.* One student insisted that Mrs. Mitty was meddlesome and annoying; while another countered that she was a caring wife, only concerned for their safety.

### *Activating and Engaging*
The team will examine an aggregate of eighth-grade performance graphed by each of the six writing traits and based on a four-point scale. Before looking at the results, the team members discuss their predictions and assumptions. As one team member charts assumptions, another records predictions using a blank graph that mirrors the format of the data they are about to explore.

> "Kids have been drilled in grammar, punctuation, and capitalization since third grade. So, I think that more than 60 percent of our students will score at 3 or more on conventions."

"I'm not sure that will play out for this assignment, because these kids spend more time texting, which has its own set of conventions. Given that, I think only 25 to 30 percent will score at above expectation."

This dialogue continues as group members share predictions and assumptions until each trait has been discussed and the blank chart is complete.

### Exploring and Discovering

The team sits in a semicircle oriented toward an enlarged graph of the performance results. Everyone takes a minute to silently view the display. Some teachers jot down observations that stand out to them. Others glance back and forth between the predictions graph and the formal results. After this purposeful pause, the conversation begins with one team member moving to a chart stand to record her observations.

"Check this out; the scores for voice are higher than I thought they'd be. It looks like 37 percent of the kids scored a 3 or better on that trait."

"There appears to be a pattern here. The scores for word choice, sentence fluency, and ideas are all within 5 percent of one another—ranging from 53 to 58 percent."

"Given our differing views of how they'd do on conventions, it's interesting to see that 41 percent scored a 3 or better in that area."

The dialogue continues as the team considers the data for each trait, noting any surprise and searching for comparisons and contrasts between the bars for each writing strand. Though tempted, the members are careful not to move to explanation or conclusions at this point.

### Organizing and Integrating

After thoughtful data exploration, the recorder circles two observations the team chooses as focal points for generating theories of causation. The specific observations caught the team's attention as areas for improving writing performance on the next benchmark assessment. Based on these observations, team members begin to generate causal theories.

"I think the reason that 55 percent of the kids scored well on ideas is because the kids related to the story, and we used discussion protocols before the writing assessment. Let's explore that further and see if it also holds for sentence fluency and word choice."

"My theory is that the higher scores in word choice are because in our middle school program, we teach some of these skills more thoroughly and consistently from grade to grade than others. For example, I think we all work hard at emphasizing vocabulary in our language arts lessons."

At that point, the team subdivides into two working groups to clarify the data needed to confirm or modify each of these working theories.

• • • • • • • • • • • • • • • • • • • • • • • • • • • • • • • • • • • • •

## Exercise Your Learning

Work with a data team of four to six participants, and prepare a small sample of relevant student data. Apply the collaborative learning cycle in the following seven ways.

1. Invite the group to predict areas of success and its assumptions related to these.

2. Post the data sample, and engage in the exploring and discovering process.

3. Circle items that indicate specific areas of success in this data sample.

4. Generate theories of causation that support these observations.

5. Identify additional data sources to confirm and clarify these causal theories.

6. Generalize from the patterns of success, and consider other areas in which these patterns might apply.

7. Save time to reflect on the process. Use the Reflecting on Your Experience reproducible.

## Extend Your Learning

The National School Reform Faculty site (www.nsrfharmony.org/resources .html) presents a wealth of resources and protocols for group work.

The Looking at Student Work website (www.lasw.org) offers a collection of protocols and tips for helping groups examine student work.

TimerTools™ (www.kaganonline.com/catalog/ETT) is a software-based timer for digital projection. It supports Windows and Macintosh operating systems. Public timers help group members stay on task and guide for self-pacing.

# Reflecting on Your Experience

Reflecting on this experience, what are some of the things you noticed about yourself, your group, the structure, and the process? Write your responses in the following chart.

| Yourself | Your Group |
|---|---|
|  |  |
| **The Structure** | **The Process** |
|  |  |

Based on this experience, what are some of the things that you want to be aware of as you continue to apply the collaborative learning cycle?

# CHAPTER THREE

# *Avoiding Reality Wars*

Our ways of viewing the world both empower and trap us. These mental maps have a profound influence on what we see, how we see, and how we make sense of things. While they help us make sense, they also impair our capacity for open-minded exploration. The caution is that we do not let our preferences become our prescriptions. Well-structured data-based investigations reduce certainty, promoting a spirit of inquiry as groups engage in framing problems and seeking solutions. As former U.S. Senator Daniel Moynihan has said, "You're entitled to your own opinion, but you're not entitled to your own facts" (Greenspan, 2007, p. 95).

Mental models are tenacious and often remain hidden from view. This tendency to stubbornly hold on to unexplored perspectives and beliefs is compounded by the social, emotional, and cognitive complexity of working in groups. Skillful application of the collaborative learning cycle keeps groups and group members open to surprise, producing purposeful uncertainty and conscious curiosity.

Nevertheless, even with scaffolds, structures, and skills, groups still struggle when working with data. Long-held patterns of reasoning by anecdote and persuading by volume and repetition inhibit open-minded exploration. The need for group members to convince others of the "correct way" to see data, or solve a problem, creates tension and drains time and energy from group work. The tendency to selectively choose data as evidence produces a dynamic of confirming beliefs instead of exploring issues. The trap here is using data to prove instead of to improve.

> *The tendency to selectively choose data as evidence produces a dynamic of confirming beliefs instead of exploring issues. The trap here is using data to prove instead of to improve.*

## Pursuing Meaningful Data

Avoiding these reality wars, or polarized conversations, requires thoughtful framing of issues—determining the necessary data sources for well-structured explorations and agreements about the focus and responsibility of the group's work.

The data pursuit begins with a design choice. Two distinct pathways are open for this purpose: (1) starting with data or (2) starting with an issue. Either choice is equally effective. In either case, the potential for reality wars is always present. When starting with the data, the choice of data, the validity of the assessments that produced the data, and the use of vibrant data displays are all important considerations. For example, the data may be given to a team by a district superintendent or someone external to the team, who has already analyzed it and delivered a mandate for improvement; or it may be the result of the team's application of the collaborative learning cycle and identification of focus areas.

Alternatively, an issue might emerge at a staff meeting, via action research, or even during informal discussions about student observations or classroom practices. When starting with an issue, clarifying just what the real issue *is* and establishing its priority level for the group's attention increase the engagement and thoughtful participation of group members.

In this case, the data pursuit will be organized according to how the issue is framed. Three effective ways to frame the exploration are (1) constructing a problem statement, (2) crafting an inquiry, or (3) generating a hypothesis. The best choice is determined by the context or nature of the specific issue. In many cases, it is helpful to have the group generate an example of each way to frame a specific issue to see which way captures the essential nature of the concern and might best focus the group's exploration of that issue.

## Constructing a Problem Statement

Complaints spew out at group meetings with high frequency. Transforming complaints into problem statements can energize a group to assume collective responsibility and to engage with the issue as a data-based exploration. Shared problem definitions are critical to success, yet can be challenging to develop. The problem statement drives the data quest and frames the theory of action. Thoughtfully constructing problem statements helps a group to sort peripheral issues from those that are central to study. Effectively completing the stem "The problem is _____" appears deceptively simple on the surface, but in practice may take a whole meeting to complete.

For example, concern about students completing their homework, or even doing their assignments at all, might arise during a team meeting. To construct an effective problem statement, the issue needs to be defined and refined. What patterns does the team see? Are there certain types of assignments, days of the week, or subject areas that jump out? With the group's careful examination, a clear problem statement emerges, and a worthwhile data pursuit ensues. Note the evolution of the problem statements in table 3.1.

## Crafting an Inquiry

Similarly, groups can construct a concern as a question—provided there are no preferred answers. Recasting concerns and observations as inquiries opens up the potential solution set, widens the possibilities, and keeps certainty at bay. Groups using well-formed inquiries embrace *both/and* thinking and avoid

**Table 3.1: Developing Problem Statements**

| Initial Problem Statement | Refined Problem Statement |
|---|---|
| The problem is that the kids don't all turn in their homework on time. | The problem is that some of our students do not see a connection between the homework we assign and successful learning. |
| The problem is that there is really low performance in ninth-grade math. | The problem is that incoming freshmen do not have the basic computation skills for success, and we aren't adjusting our instruction to meet their needs. |
| The problem is that kids don't have any respect. | The problem is students don't have clear models of expected behavior or consistently applied consequences for misbehaving. |

the traps of *either/or* thinking. For example, inquiries regarding homework might include, "What are some differences between students who complete their homework and those who don't?" "What might be some causal factors that keep students from successful homework completion?" "Considering specific students, what percentage of the time do they complete (or not complete) their assignments?" "How can we determine students' readiness for successful independent practice?"

## *Generating a Hypothesis*

Solutions frequently emerge from conversations steeped in anecdotes and observations. Competing solutions can be sources of tension that result in debate or withdrawal. Those with the greatest passion or energy about an issue often impose solutions that not all group members may understand or own. Reframing solutions as hypotheses creates a path for shared exploration and converts a reality war into a data-team study. Hypotheses often have an if/then format. For example, "If we provided more guided practice and used formative assessment to determine readiness, then students would have the confidence to complete their homework assignments successfully." "If the homework was clearly related to the following day's instruction, then students would be more likely to come prepared." "If we provided choice in assignments, such as how many or which examples to complete, then students would be more likely to complete their homework." Well-constructed frames focus and facilitate the next stages of the group's work—selecting, gathering, and exploring the data.

The key to a productive investigation and ultimately an effective improvement plan is root-cause analysis. We need to know what is causing the present results before moving to potential plans for improvement.

# Searching for Root Causes

In most cases, the problems worth pursuing are messy. They require thoughtful analysis, not impulsive action. Groups often go for the quick fix, treating surface symptoms rather than searching for the deeper causal factors, but the root causes of the current levels of student performance are deep, underlying factors.

*Root causes are the story beneath the story. They are resistant to short-term or simple remediation.*

Root causes are the story beneath the story. They are resistant to short-term or simple remediation. When exploring data, the question groups first need to ask is not, "What steps do we need to take?" but rather "What is causing these results?"

Consider this scenario. A district's fourth-grade math results indicate wide gaps in problem-solving performance. Some teachers are convinced that basic computation skills are the cause of the deficits. A supplementary push-in program to improve computation skills is proposed. However, upon further examination of additional data, including students' daily work and their performance in other content areas, the group discovers reading comprehension and math-specific vocabulary as the primary causal factors. Ultimately, the improvement plan focuses on reading and reasoning skills across content areas.

Determining root cause is critical to school improvement, particularly when there are tenacious patterns of low performance. These patterns might appear for content areas, specific skills, learning outcomes, student populations, grade levels, specific teachers, or schools within a district. Several factors compound the complexity of determining root causes. Individual teachers often have too narrow a lens if their own classrooms are the only perspective available to them. The opportunity for pattern seeking, which requires a wide, broad, or high view of results, is limited unless teachers are working collaboratively. Even then, the team's work culture, as described in chapter 1, determines its capacity for vigorous inquiry, sustained focus, and open, honest, data-centered conversations. These skills are necessary to dig deep and push past the comfort of a quick fix.

## Distinguishing Correlation From Causation

Simply because there is a correlation between events, behaviors, or results does not necessarily mean there is causality. For example, suppose middle school teachers report that more students are completing their homework more of the time. At the same time, the school has ramped up the negative consequence for not handing in assignments; specifically, it added a supervised study hall and a detention period. Teachers speculate that this improvement in homework completion is based on the new program. However, teachers don't know if the result is causal without additional exploration. It is also possible that the students' mandated participation in study hall has captured parental attention, which has driven consequences at home that have produced a higher degree of homework completion.

It is important to distinguish between causality and correlation, if we ultimately want more or less of the same results. That is, to increase your currently positive results or decrease your currently negative results, you have to know first what's really causing the results. In this case, if parent engagement rather than school-based punishment is key to success, then outreach to families would be high on the list of the school's interventions.

# Pursuing Worthy Problems

There is no shortage of problems in any school setting. Groups need to be selective in where and how they will focus their time and energy. Reality wars may erupt when conflicting perspectives surface. Groups can get sidetracked when advocacy for personal pet peeves dominates the conversation. For cohesive and productive work, groups need shared criteria to define, agree on, and prioritize which problems to take on.

## *Deciding When a Problem Is a Worthy Problem*

Given all the possibilities for a group's attention and energy, the following criteria can support the decision of what issues might be worth pursuing.

- An issue recurs with frequency, year after year.

- An issue is pervasive across multiple grade levels, student groups, or school settings.

- An issue consumes high levels of energy, time, and resources.

- Even after an improvement bump, performance plateaus and subsequent data flatline.

Consider the following examples.

- For the last four years, a high school's algebra results have consistently been 35–45 percent lower than the language arts scores for the same students on the annual statewide assessment. Each year, members of the math team suggest various solutions such as after-school homework support programs, test-preparation classes, different grouping strategies, and alterations in the instructional sequence. After four years, no significant improvements have occurred.

- In all four elementary schools in a large urban district, there is a strong improvement trend in elementary reading scores in the primary grades. Intense professional development activities, skillful literacy coaches, and innovative student-grouping patterns are all credited with contributing to this success. Unfortunately, in grades 4 and 5, scores are stagnating and showing little growth from year to year for the same period. Committees are searching for new teaching materials, developing student skills assessments, and proposing longer language arts teaching blocks.

- English learners are showing positive results in the primary-grade mathematics. In fact, math and language arts scores are showing steady improvement gains, and the achievement gap with native speakers is steadily shrinking. From grades 4 to 8, these math gains disappear, with scores showing year-to-year decline as students get older. Group members have many conflicting causality theories about the decrease in performance. Some think that the causes are essentially language based; some think that it is a matter of student motivation; others argue for expanding instructional approaches.

Each of these examples meets the criteria for worthy problems and has the potential to consume considerable time, energy, and resources. These examples are also complex, with no apparent or straightforward solutions. When the underlying causal factors are not clear, group members often lack confidence and commitment to proposed solutions. The extra time required to search for and clarify the root causes of problems is time well spent.

## Identifying Causal Theories

A theory is a way of viewing the world. *Theory* has the same Greek root, *theoros*, as the word *theater*. Individual group members bring their own theories of a problem with related possible solutions to the table. These potentially conflicting views can create tensions, disagreement, and loss of focus in group work. Persistent problems are often the result of shallow causal theories and quick-fix solutions.

Our perspectives on a problem stem from our frames of reference and are informed by technical knowledge, past experiences, and personal successes. As introduced in chapter 2 (pages 33–34), five causal categories seem to hold most problem frames and solution sets: curriculum, instruction, teachers, students, and infrastructure. (See figure 3.1.)

1.  **Curriculum:** Design and implementation
2.  **Instruction:** Methods, materials, and resources
3.  **Teachers:** Knowledge, skills, and dispositions
4.  **Students:**  Knowledge, skills, and dispositions
5.  **Infrastructure:** Schedules, programming, and resources

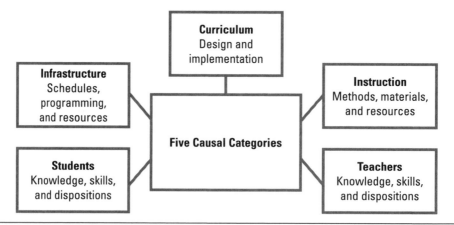

**Figure 3.1: Five causal categories for problem frames and solution sets.**

Premature certainty stalls groups when individual group members lock onto a preferred causal theory, obscuring other possibilities. Pushing for multiple theories of causation reduces some of these blocks and helps widen the individual and collective perspectives on the issue. These theories then become hypotheses for testing with additional data before developing action plans.

For example, in the high school algebra dilemma, described previously as a *worthy problem*, the data suggest several potential causal categories for exploration.

- **Student knowledge, skills, and dispositions:** To what degree are students entering high school with strong foundations in fundamental mathematical skills, such as basic arithmetic operations and knowledge of fractions, percentages, and ratios? What are ways that students perceive the processes of learning math, and what might motivate them to engage more deeply?

- **Curriculum design and implementation:** Which parts of this issue are directly related to the algebra program at the high school? To what degree is there consistency and fidelity to the written curriculum? Do all teachers using similar topic sequences get similar results?

- **Teacher knowledge, skills, and dispositions:** How confident are algebra teachers in their content knowledge and instructional approaches? To what degree do they believe that their students have the capabilities to achieve high levels of mathematical knowledge and skills?

Note: As in this example, not all five causal categories will be involved when generating causal theories. Often, one or two are the major drivers for further exploration.

## *Choosing Data*

There may be more than one root cause for an event or a problem, and there will likely be multiple contributory factors. Each theory requires additional data, inquiry, and dialogue to refine the picture of underlying causes and reveal the patterns that are producing the current discouraging results. The challenging work is summoning the energy and sustaining the effort required to explore multiple causal theories before generating solutions.

Once several causal theories emerge, the question becomes, Which data sources are necessary to clarify and develop agreement on the main drivers? Ultimately, the tentative causal theory will determine which data to collect and examine in future sessions. (See chapter 4, page 54.)

## *Building Collective Responsibility*

The habits of root-cause analysis transform reactive cultures into forward-looking cultures, developing solutions that foster and sustain growth over time. Well-structured, shared exploration extinguishes the backward-blame game ("What am I supposed to do? They should've learned that last year"). Messy problems belong to all of us. One grade, grade level, content area, or classroom does not own them.

*Reality wars also include battles over the best solutions. Personal preferences and passions polarize groups, allying some group members while alienating others.*

Reality wars also include battles over the best solutions. Personal preferences and passions polarize groups, allying some group members while alienating others. You can't sell solutions to people who don't own the problem or define it in the same way. When group members collaboratively grapple with and agree on the problem definition, there is greater collective commitment to the subsequent action plan.

Once a direction is established, productive groups use their meetings and classrooms as laboratories for learning. They monitor progress by collecting artifacts and performance data to share with one another. Following through on these commitments results in deeper relational trust and a greater belief in the power of collaborative practice—and multiple experiences of this nature produce higher degrees of collective efficacy.

## • • • • • • • • Data Story: Finding the Starting Point • • • • • • • •

It is January at Springfield High School, and the language arts learning team is meeting to review the midterm exams. As the team members dig into the data, they all agree that a clear pattern emerges regarding the tenth graders' comprehension skills, especially when it comes to informational or expository text.

Each team member feels sure about what to do, and a lively discussion ensues.

"The problem here is that the kids are not strategic readers. They just don't have the comprehension skills they need to understand text at this level—especially in the content areas."

"Well, the real problem is they enter high school without those skills, and without any way to develop them, they fall further and further behind."

"Maybe, but then we have to ask what the differences are between those kids who are skillful and those who aren't. Maybe see if they came from the same middle schools, or see what kind of recreational reading they do—if any."

"I don't know if any of that matters. At this point, we need to help them increase their reading skills. If students are presented with multiple opportunities for guided reading of informational texts in all of the content areas, then they would be more competent as independent readers."

"Well, I think before we can address the issue, we need more information. We should be reasonably confident about what's causing these results before we start changing instructional practice, especially if we want to recruit our content-area colleagues."

"Agreed. So, what do we need to explore?"

"Minimally, we should look at some other assessment instruments to see if the patterns persist. Right now, we're just looking at our district test. We can tap the state scores and also take a closer look at our unit assessments."

"Right, and how about talking with students, maybe a random sample, to see how they feel about reading, and what they read outside of class, and maybe other ways they interact with text-based information?"

"We could also give the kids a quick reading assessment based on something current and relevant to their lives, like that article about cell phone use and the effect on the brain, and see how they do with that."

The team agrees to take a deeper look, and the meeting ends with determining how it will gather the additional data and how data will be organized for an efficient cross-check before determining solutions.

• • • • • • • • • • • • • • • • • • • • • • • • • • • • • • • • • • • • • • • •

# Exercise Your Learning

Use the Choosing Which Data to Collect reproducible (page 51, or online at **go.solution-tree.com/teams**) to explore something in your work setting you are interested in knowing more about. Work independently, with a partner, or as a team.

# Extend Your Learning

The Mind Tools website offers a variety of practical tools for problem solving, planning, and decision making. Explore the "5 Whys" (Mind Tools, n.d.c) protocol for quickly getting to the root of a problem (www.mindtools.com /pages/article/newTMC_5W.htm). The site also offers links to articles about root cause analysis and cause-effect analysis.

A "5 Whys Root Cause Analysis" (Integrated Performance Leadership Group [IPL], 2007) worksheet is available from the IPL Group website (www .theiplgroup.com/5%20Whys%20Template.pdf). This simple graphic tool offers a visual guide to the "5 Whys" question process.

To learn how to develop fishbone or cause-and-effect diagrams, view this short video tutorial (www.youtube.com/watch?v=bNDlg1h-za0), which explains how to construct the diagrams showing the causal factors that may be producing an outcome or problem (Hajek, 2009).

Visit the American Society for Quality (ASQ) website to learn about Pareto charts (http://asq.org/learn-about-quality/cause-analysis-tools/overview/pareto .html). Pareto charts are helpful for analyzing data about the frequency of problems and searching for underlying causes. They support groups in determining which situations or factors are most significant. Pareto is the source of the well-known 80/20 rule, which states that 80 percent of the benefits will result from 20 percent of the efforts, or 80 percent of the problems come from 20 percent of the causes. The key is determining and targeting the 20 percent (ASQ, n.d.).

Bright Hub (McDonough, 2011) offers a tutorial illustrating the steps in creating Pareto charts in Excel (www.brighthub.com/office/project-management /articles/8708.aspx).

# Choosing Which Data to Collect

1. Identify something in your own work setting that you are interested in knowing more about (such as a curriculum gap, an instructional gap, a student skill deficit, or a student behavioral pattern).

   *Example: High school student skills with reading informational text*

   Your issue: _____

   _____


2. To explore this issue, craft examples of each of the following.

   **A problem statement:** The problem is _____.

   *Example: The problem is that students do not apply effective reading strategies to understand informational text.*

   Your problem statement: _____

   _____


   **An inquiry:** How are we doing with _____? What are the essential differences between _____ and _____? Why does _____? What are the most productive _____?

   *Example: What are the essential differences between students who are skillful readers of informational text and those who are not?*

   Your inquiry: _____

   _____

   _____


   **A hypothesis:** If _____ then _____.

   *Example: If students are presented with multiple opportunities for guided reading of informational texts, then students will be more successful in transferring these skills to independent practice.*

   Your hypothesis: _____

   _____

   _____

   _____

page 1 of 2

3. Determine which framing structure might be the most productive to explore (problem statement, inquiry, or hypothesis).

Your framing structure: _____


4. Identify at least three data sources you might tap to gather additional information about your issue.

*Examples:*

> *a. State or provincial and local reading assessment data*
>
> *b. Interviews with skillful teachers to determine which reading skills they deem to be the most essential*
>
> *c. Samples of students' written responses to informational text*

Your data sources: _____

_____

_____

_____

# CHAPTER FOUR

# Knowing the Data Fundamentals

Data literacy can be inert—a skill for understanding and describing data—or active—a vital method for generating a knowledge source that informs action. With purposeful identification, collection, examination, and interpretation, data become energizing sources of information. Data options to explore extend beyond quantitative, wide-scaled measures, such as state achievement tests, and include a variety of both formative and summative sources. When groups collaboratively explore the data, rich conversations produce new understandings for group members about their students, their practice, their programs, and themselves.

Prodding, poking, and inquiring into what's going on, why it's going on, and whether it is satisfactory motivates change. A rigorous, data-driven process allows practitioners to better describe the current state of achievement and to identify gaps between the present state and their desired achievement outcomes. Potential gaps might exist between individual students' or groups'

> *Prodding, poking, and inquiring into what's going on, why it's going on, and whether it is satisfactory motivates change.*

achievement and the high expectations we set for them, between a particular program's or curriculum's effectiveness and the standards we identify for successful implementation, and between one school's performance and another's. The collaborative learning cycle provides a framework for structuring productive, time-efficient, and balanced conversations.

This chapter explains data fundamentals—data types, sources, terms, and tools—to support groups in effectively implementing the collaborative learning cycle and to broaden perspectives on the types of data that might further their work. Schools and school districts are rich in data. Determining how much and what types of data will best serve collaborative inquiry and the group's ultimate outcomes is critical to effective application of the collaborative learning cycle. It is important that the data involved provide both a broad and a deep view of the present picture but are not so complex that the process becomes overwhelming and unmanageable. By examining multiple sources of data, groups glean insights from several angles on the issues under study.

## Two Types of Data: Qualitative and Quantitative

Fundamentally, there are two major types of data: (1) qualitative and (2) quantitative. Qualitative data rely on description, while quantitative data rely on numbers.

Qualitative data tend to be narrative, holistic, and longitudinal. Schools may gather qualitative data from the classroom, grade, department, or school level. Classroom-, grade level–, or department-based data include anecdotal records, student work samples, portfolios, student interviews, checklists, and homework assignments. School-level data include meeting agendas, teacher demographics (years of experience, education, and so on), memos, schedules, and curriculum maps.

Quantitative data are expressed numerically and statistically. Quantitative sources include test scores of all types, performance grades, attendance records, and enrollment data. Quantitative results are intended for comparisons between students, groups of students, schools, districts, states or provinces, and nations. Thus, they are expressed and described using stanines, quartiles, norm-curve equivalents, means, medians, and modes.

Each type of data is organized differently for analysis. Because quantitative data use numbers, percentiles, and other mathematical configurations, and they are organized based on frequency distributions, central tendencies, variabilities, and dispersions, it is easier to create tables, charts, and graphs to discuss and analyze quantitative data. For example, isolating, or disaggregating, norm-referenced test scores by variables such as gender, race, or socioeconomic status allows teams to identify relationships and patterns within the blur of numbers.

Qualitative data, which are descriptive, are usually reviewed holistically through examining anecdotes and artifacts. For comparative purposes and to discern patterns or trends, teams can organize these sources by frequency of instances, events, responses, products, or so on. Teams can use the categories or topics that emerge from the individual items identified for tables, charts, or further investigation. For example, by logging discipline issues by type, time of year, time of day, and school location, teams discover relationships from the flow of events that are often unseen by those too close to the individual occurrences.

It is important to note that while numbers are often used for scoring qualitative assessment, for example in rubrics and survey scales, that does not mean the data are quantitative. These numbers provide relative, and still often subjective, comparisons that rely on individual judgment. They do not provide data that are statistically comparable. Table 4.1 provides some examples of quantitative and qualitative data.

**Table 4.1: Examples of Quantitative and Qualitative Data**

|  | Quantitative Data | Qualitative Data |
|---|---|---|
| **Student Performance Data** | A variety of test results including proficiency tests, standardized tests, state exams, district, and classroom-based tests<br><br>Report card grades<br><br>The number of students receiving special services from local, state, or federal resources<br><br>Attendance rates, mobility rates, expulsion rates, suspension rates, or dropout rates<br><br>Percentage of high school graduates<br><br>Percentage of students with disabilities who are mainstreamed into regular classes<br><br>Percentage of retentions or advancements | Student portfolios and other work products<br><br>Videotapes of student work and performances<br><br>Exhibitions<br><br>Student surveys, including pleasure-reading inventories, self-esteem stems, and self-assessment profiles<br><br>Student journals and learning logs<br><br>Observational records, anecdotal records, and running records<br><br>Student interviews<br><br>Checklists |
| **Program Data** | Teacher-student ratios<br><br>Numbers of students enrolled in various programs like advanced placement<br><br>Head Start, all-day kindergarten, and prevention and intervention programs<br><br>Teacher and administrator education statistics, for example, education levels achieved, average number of years with district, average number of years of service overall, number of inductees (first three years), and number of retirements expected in the next three years<br><br>Teacher participation in professional development activities<br><br>Budget and resource allocations | Videotapes of special events, classrooms, and hallways<br><br>Meeting agendas, minutes, and memos<br><br>Teacher and administrator portfolios<br><br>Artifacts like awards and photos of bulletin boards<br><br>Staff interviews<br><br>Workshop and training program agendas and evaluations<br><br>Bulletins and newsletters |
| **Community Data** | Data on family demographics, for example, average income, percentage of single-parent families, and percentage of two-income households<br><br>Number of school and business and industry partnerships<br><br>Employment rate; employment sectors in the area | Focus-group data<br><br>Opinion surveys<br><br>Interviews with parents and community members |

*Source: Wellman & Lipton, 2004.*

## Formative and Summative Data

Both quantitative and qualitative data can be used formatively or summatively. Formative data illuminate what students know and can do and what they cannot yet do. Using data formatively provides feedback for teachers and learners to inform next steps and potential instructional modifications. Summative data are used to make judgments about student learning, effective instruction, or the effectiveness of a program or plan, generally at the end of an instructional period.

> *Formative data illuminate what students know and can do and what they cannot yet do. . . . Summative data are used to make judgments about student learning, effective instruction, or the effectiveness of a program or plan.*

### Formative Assessment

Dylan Wiliam (2011) offers a comprehensive definition of formative assessment that includes the work of several others in the field. Each description includes three fundamental aspects. Formative assessment (1) involves both teachers and students, (2) provides feedback for teachers to modify instructional activities, and (3) is applied during the instructional process for the purpose of improvement. Formative assessment is also process oriented. Various tools, instruments, and strategies are used to provide feedback based on the interaction between teacher and student, student and student, and student and information or learning task. It is active, responsive, and adaptable. The information provided is just as important for the students as it is for the teachers, if not more so.

When teachers collaboratively explore formative assessment data, they can look for patterns and determine adjustments in teaching to improve learning. Through regular, ongoing monitoring and then focusing interventions and adjustments accordingly, teachers optimize student learning and increase student performance on summative measures that determine judgments about performance, programs, and practitioners.

### Summative Assessment

Teachers collect summative data in short cycles at the end of instruction, as in benchmark data, or at the end of a course. Summative assessment can be quantitative, such as unit tests and state or provincial exams, or qualitative, such as rubric-driven projects or student portfolios.

It is best to use summative data to make decisions about curriculum, to direct future instruction, and to improve professional practice. Often, teachers use yearly summative data to begin a collaborative learning cycle and apply identified formative sources at appropriate intervals for continuous improvement.

## Reliability, Validity, and Credibility

Here we offer definitions and distinctions between several terms related to data. While *reliability* and *validity* tend to be terms applied to quantitative data, the concept of *trustworthiness*, or *dependability*, is still important when considering data sources and results. The concern for confidence in the findings brings the idea of *credibility* to the forefront. Whether or not results are considered reliable, valid, trustworthy, or dependable is often subjective and is more about the viewer than the viewed.

## Reliability

Reliability refers to consistent measures or results from a particular tool or instrument. An instrument is considered reliable if it produces the same result time after time. For example, if a test is designed to measure computation skills for first graders, then each time the test is administered to first graders it should produce essentially the same results. The concern for reliability is one reason that schools tend to rely heavily on norm- and criterion-referenced tests. These measures are generally reliable across time and for a wide range of students. However, the test items are limited regarding what they can measure, as they are designed to fit a neutral, objective machine-scoring system. Open-ended questions—those requiring responses that show inventiveness, creativity, or examples intended to reveal the process of problem solving—do not fit these systems. While more authentic measures, such as performance tasks and portfolios, can provide data on these skills and attributes, they raise the problem of *inter-rater reliability*. This problem occurs when different scorers arrive at different results, or when an individual scorer's ratings over time show wide differentiation. Failure to invest time and energy in developing shared performance standards and scoring accuracy reduces the effectiveness and credibility of performance tasks. Scoring rubrics, exemplars, and training sessions designed to increase inter-rater reliability are intended to reduce this concern.

## Validity

While reliability is concerned with the accuracy of the instrument based on the consistency of results, validity refers to the degree to which an instrument measures what it is designed to measure—that the data reflect what they are intended to show. For example, many fill-in and multiple-choice tests are intended to measure content knowledge, but may be more likely to measure a student's syntactical knowledge or reading ability. One subset of validity regards content. *Content validity* indicates how comprehensively an instrument measures or completely tests for the domain of knowledge it is intended to assess. For example, using an assessment that only includes items that test decoding to determine comprehension skills would indicate a lack of content validity as the broad range of comprehension skills would not be measured.

Further, although standardized, norm-referenced tests are highly reliable, they may not be valid in measuring sophisticated conceptual understanding, or the ability to solve complex problems. Such tests may also contain questions that permit students to be credited with correct answers for the wrong reason, give away the answer in the options presented in multiple-choice questions, or contain language that is linguistically or culturally confusing to students. (For insight into this issue and specific examples, visit http://marciakastner.com/10 -common-flaws-in-math-tests_289.html; Kastner, 2009a).

### Credibility

An additional concern when considering what data to explore is that of credibility. An individual's experiences, knowledge, and confidence using different data tools will influence his or her perception of its believability, or credibility. No matter how reliable and valid an instrument may be, differences in learning style and educational philosophy, as well as diversity in gender, ethnicity, professional position, and so on, influence a group member's approach to and participation in data-driven inquiry. By incorporating multiple data types and multiple sources in a data exploration—qualitative and quantitative, classroom-centered, and systems-based assessments—leaders will ensure that more group members can relate to more of the data. In other words, the data are more credible because they are within the scope of individual group member's readiness to accept them.

# Triangulation and Disaggregation

Both triangulation and disaggregation give data teams clearer and more precise information from which to work. *Triangulation* is an effective method for increasing credibility and dependability when in a data exploration. Imagine that an event occurs in a central plaza between three buildings. In each building, there is someone at a window watching the scene unfold. No single perspective could offer a full picture of what occurred. To get a comprehensive description, information from each of the three observers is needed. When exploring data, the same concept applies. Triangulation requires multiple views, or multiple sources, to create a more complete assessment of the issue being studied.

*Disaggregation*, or breaking a large swatch of data into smaller subsets, often reveals what may remain hidden or buried. Discerning the part from the whole gives a more precise view of those parts and often reveals more information about the underlying issues within the larger whole.

## Using Multiple Sources: Triangulation

No individual assessment or measurement instrument is a perfect fit for providing what we want to know about whom and in what ways. Using multiple data sources compensates for the deficits in individual tools and provides a comprehensive picture of the topic under study. Together, these data sources provide a more comprehensive picture than any individual data set could. *Triangulation* is a researcher's term for taking at least three different perspectives on an area of study.

One view alone offers a limited and usually too narrow viewpoint. For example, standardized test scores for School A indicate that 64 percent of the students in grade 8 scored proficient or above on the state language arts exam. A performance ranking of the eighth-grade students reveals a clearer understanding of where within each band these students performed. Demographic data on each of the students offer even more information about groups that may be marginalized, or specific cohorts whose learning needs are not being met. Triangulation is one way of addressing validity. We can reasonably assume that if three different measures are all indicating similar results, they offer valid information regarding what we want to know.

Triangulating the data is most powerful when the various sources are diverse and varied. Thus, a qualitative measure such as a student survey will enhance quantitative measures like state or provincial exams. A third source that is different from either of these, such as teacher anecdotes or a curriculum map, can enhance the view. The idea is to seek multiple sources, using different methods and operating at different levels or in different areas of the school. This approach also addresses credibility in that multiple sources of differing data types are most likely to be credible to different group members. Intentionally seeking multiple perspectives, both of the data and those analyzing them, enriches the process and outcomes.

## Making the Invisible Visible: Disaggregation

*Disaggregation* is breaking the data apart and reorganizing it into smaller subsets. These data might be subscores within a larger measure. For example, disaggregated scores are often provided for criterion- and norm-referenced tests by skill strands. In addition to the total reading score, the results provide a look at literal and inferential comprehension or vocabulary skills. Or data might be disaggregated based on a specific characteristic, such as viewing math scores by gender or exploring for correlations between reading performance and specific socioeconomic groups.

Disaggregation addresses important questions about what is working (or not) and for whom. For example, disaggregating data by gender helps determine whether an improvement in math achievement reflects equal gains for male and female students. The same questions can be explored for any subset to determine and ensure that all students have equal access and opportunity to learn.

Disaggregated data give much clearer, more specific information than holistic, blanket scores. Keep in mind that there are subsets within subsets. It is important to sort a variety of variables, but not so many that the data become overwhelmingly complex or that the subgroup becomes too small.

Data that are disaggregated by race or ethnicity, gender, income, academic programs, geographic area, feeder schools, and even classroom teachers will often reveal patterns and provide indicators of present and potential future performance that remain hidden in large data lumps.

# Dimensions of Data

To choose data is also to choose perspective. Just as the vista from the top of the mountain is quite different than the view from the valley, varied data offer varied lenses on the world of learning.

*To choose data is also to choose perspective. . . . Varied data offer varied lenses on the world of learning.*

## Information Altitudes

One important dimension of data is its distance in time or level from the topic under study. Different types of data offer wide-angle or telephoto images of student performance. For example, to explore middle school students' achievement in science, the data might include individual student scores, grade-level scores, schoolwide scores, and perhaps districtwide scores. Each set of scores might include normed indices, such as the Northwest Evaluation Association Measures of Academic Progress (MAP) or the Trends in International Mathematics and Science Study (TIMSS), provincial- or state-level scores measuring provincial or state standards, as well as district, school, department, or classroom-based tests. In addition, data might include student work samples, homework assignments, projects, journals, or portfolios. We think of these measures based on their distance from the initial inquiry and the dimensions of the field of focus. If investigating the question, How are our students performing in science at the middle school level?, the individual student work would offer the closest view, while the nationally or internationally referenced tests, the farthest. (See figure 4.1 for an example.)

## Temporal Dimension

Data also have a temporal dimension. That is, we can explore data that have been archived from past events, we can observe and collect present samples, and we can project measurements and tools that will yield information into the future. Once again, if we're interested in exploring the effectiveness of our science instruction, we can look at standardized achievement scores for the previous three years to surface trend data (past). We can also conduct surveys regarding students' attitudes toward science and demographic data about the science teachers (present). In addition, we can identify data that will be useful when they become available, such as scores on end-of-grade tests or state science exams (future).

## Specific Questions

A question-driven approach is a powerful way to motivate and mobilize energy for school improvement. Questions related to differences, similarities, gaps, qualities, characteristics (both desired and existing), patterns of success, impact of programs, curriculum, instructional methods, and so on provide relevant starting points for a data pursuit. This approach is true whether the questions emerge from a data exploration or provide the impetus to begin one.

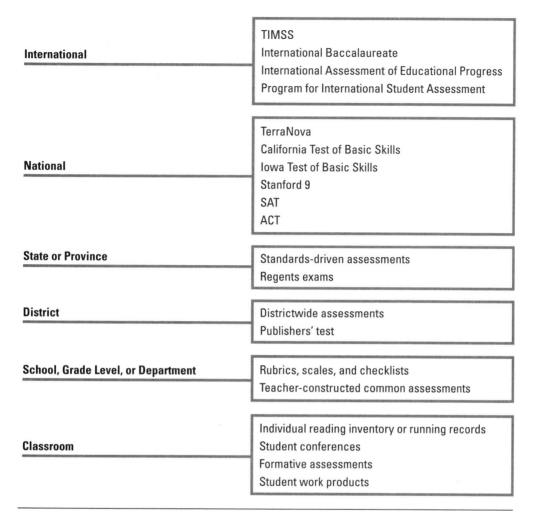

| International | TIMSS<br>International Baccalaureate<br>International Assessment of Educational Progress<br>Program for International Student Assessment |
| National | TerraNova<br>California Test of Basic Skills<br>Iowa Test of Basic Skills<br>Stanford 9<br>SAT<br>ACT |
| State or Province | Standards-driven assessments<br>Regents exams |
| District | Districtwide assessments<br>Publishers' test |
| School, Grade Level, or Department | Rubrics, scales, and checklists<br>Teacher-constructed common assessments |
| Classroom | Individual reading inventory or running records<br>Student conferences<br>Formative assessments<br>Student work products |

**Figure 4.1: Information altitudes.**

As described in chapter 3, sometimes the inquiry process begins with a question, such as, "In what ways does use of technology in the classroom affect students' research skills?," or a problem statement, such as, "Sixth-grade students enter middle school without the fundamental skills needed for proficiency in math." Or the inquiry process might begin with a hypothesis, such as, "Incidences of bullying would decrease if the curriculum included more social and emotional outcomes." Each approach still requires the identification of the data needed to explore the issue.

Another decision point involves the scope of the topic being explored. Herman and Winters (1992) describe the options as *wide angle* and *close-up*. Wide-angle investigation, whether it is at a district, school, department, or grade level, is often a good beginning for study. Close-up investigations narrow and hone the focus. For example, a district-level group might want to examine the big picture, "How effective are our science curriculum and instruction?," while a school-based team might be most interested in the question, "How has incorporating nonfiction into science units paid off for third- to fifth-grade learners?"

Wide-angle questions concern the programs' effectiveness for all learners, or large subsets. Examples of wide-angle questions include inquiry into achievement gaps among different groups in particular content areas ("Is there a positive correlation between students' skills and their performance in math? Is the rate of enrollment in advanced placement courses for minorities different than that of other groups?") or into major issues for the school population ("Is student transiency affecting graduation rates? In what ways are temporary teacher certifications affecting school discipline?").

Once a data team frames large issues and designs approaches for improvement, exploring close-up questions offers additional insights and opportunities to monitor the plan's effectiveness. Often these are the formative questions that lead to refinement and enhancement of an improvement plan. Examples in this category include questions about new methods in assessment ("How well do our new performance tasks measure our elementary students' achievement in science?") or instruction ("In what ways has differentiation improved performance for special needs students?").

*The inquiries should be clear and contextual, and they should create conscious curiosity—not fear of reprisal or evaluation.*

Most importantly, the inquiries should be clear and contextual, and they should create conscious curiosity—not fear of reprisal or evaluation. Clear questions emerge from data explorations and collaborative focus on critical issues. These inquiries often illuminate the most useful data for shedding light on areas of concern. These data choices complement and extend existing data, amplifying understanding. For example, to explore the effect of a new districtwide program on students' performance in math, we would access math achievement scores and compare the present year with the previous ones found in archival data. Data on teachers' instructional repertoire and staff participation and training outcomes for related professional development workshops would also be useful. In addition, a survey of students' perceived confidence in math or math teachers' confidence in teaching might add useful information. The workshop sign-in sheets and student and teacher surveys are examples of collectible data.

## Collectible Data Tools

Additional collection tools include checklists; anecdotal records, such as running records and teacher observation logs; videos; and charts, such as seating charts, agendas, and meeting minutes.

Collectible data usually sort into two categories: (1) behavioral and (2) perceptual. *Behavioral data*, or observational data, include the workshop sign-in sheets described previously. Other examples include frequency of office referrals or percentages of increase or decrease in parent attendance at school functions. Checklists and anecdotal records are useful instruments for collecting these data.

*Perceptual data* include interviews with various groups regarding their feelings, understandings, or opinions about a particular issue, innovation, or program. Opinions on the degree of satisfaction with the new block schedule, perceptions regarding effectiveness of the present reading program, and parents' responses to homework policy are additional examples of perceptual data. Interviews and surveys are useful tools for collecting these types of data.

## Interviews and Surveys

Protocols, such as interviews and surveys, formalize the inquiry process as instruments for data collection. The following tools are examples of commonly used methods for this purpose. An interview is essentially a survey conducted either face-to-face or via telephone. Survey instruments are generally distributed and returned electronically or through the mail, although they can be completed at a meeting. It is important to note that self-reports provide powerful perceptual data, but they are also limited in accuracy and should be triangulated with other methods.

### Interviews

Interviews are a source of qualitative, perceptual data. The intention is to record as fully and fairly as possible each respondent's particular perspective. Interpretation and analysis occur after interview data are organized—never during the interview process. It is important, therefore, to maintain a stance of inquiry when collecting interview data. Interviews vary in their degree of formality. The most informal interviews are conversational and responsive, the questions emerging from the interaction. The most formal interviews are based on carefully constructed, and often field-tested, protocols. Table 4.2 illustrates three types of interviews, ranging from least to most formal.

**Table 4.2: Three Types of Interviews**

| Interview Style | Description | Suggested Uses | Cautions |
|---|---|---|---|
| **Informal Conversational Interview** | Relies on spontaneously generating questions in the natural flow of the interaction | To explore beliefs, attitudes, values, or perceptions | Requires a high level of inquiry skills |
| **General Guided Interview** | Based on an outlined set of issues established in advance, which serves as a basic checklist to ensure all relevant topics are explored | To explore complex issues that do not have finite or predetermined responses | Requires thorough preparation<br><br>May be time consuming both in preparation and implementation |
| **Standardized Open-Ended Interview** | Consists of a carefully constructed protocol<br><br>Same sequence and wording repeats with each interviewee | To increase generalizability of results<br><br>To increase reliability and validity of research | Requires a high level of consistency<br><br>May require interviewer training |

*Source: Adapted from Wellman & Lipton, 2004.*

### Surveys

As with interviews, surveys also provide an effective method for collecting both behavioral and perceptual information. Researchers most commonly use two primary survey categories: (1) scaled and (2) unscaled.

1.  **Scaled surveys:** A scaled survey asks respondents to quantify their answers and provides information that is readily organized graphically. However, these responses are often limited in scope. For example, a response of 4 to the question, "On a scale of 1–5 how would you rate the effectiveness of this program?," does not offer information on what constitutes a 4 for this respondent, or what might have made it a 5.

2.  **Unscaled survey:** Unscaled surveys usually require responses to open-ended questions. Compared to scaled surveys, these instruments yield more potential information, but are more complex to organize for analysis. For example, a question might read, "In what ways did this program meet your expectations?" These qualitative data are most often organized into tables or charts based on emerging categories.

Creative Research Systems (2011) offers five basic steps to survey design.

1.  **Establish the goals of the project:** Determine what you want to learn or know more about.

2.  **Identify your sample:** Determine who will participate in the survey.

3.  **Choose survey methods:** Design how you will gather the information (interview or written response).

4.  **Create your questions:** Decide what you will ask and in what ways. See Types of Survey Questions (page 72) for examples. (Visit **go.solution -tree.com/teams** to download the reproducibles in this book.)

5.  **Pretest or pilot the survey:** This optional step, if practiced logistically, is useful for testing the questions, protocol, or both.

## Feasibility

*Feasibility* is the term for how realistic and reasonable it is to collect and apply a data source. The realities of life in schools create a critical need for making effective and efficient choices. Time, money, energy, and even space come into consideration in making choices about what data to collect. One tip is to look first to archival data, those things that teachers, schools, and districts are already collecting and have readily available. After tapping archival resources, groups can make creative and selective choices identifying additional collectibles that will illuminate, detail, and complement the existing data.

### Archival Data

Archival data are those that already exist and are accessible, often electronically, as part of the district's established information base. These can be both quantitative and qualitative sources. Archival data include student performance data—such as test results, grades, referral, suspension, and retention rates—and demographic data—such as percentage of students in particular programs; race, ethnicity, and gender profiles; attendance rates; and socioeconomic status (for example, numbers of students receiving free or reduced lunch). Demographic data for staff might include years of experience, types of certification, and levels of education. Mobility rates can be accessed for students, staff, and administration.

Much archival data have an anthropological quality and include sources that offer insight into the day-to-day life in the district, school, or classrooms. These data include correspondence such as memos, newsletters, bulletins, and meeting minutes; descriptions of course offerings; and available extracurricular activities. Per-pupil expenditures and other budget information fit this category, as well.

Because of its longitudinal quality, archival data can be accessed and analyzed for trends. For example, a study group might create a line graph comparing student reading scores over five years or chart the number of students participating in various extracurricular activities over a three-year period.

In addition, school archives offer access to data that relate to specific inquiries or improvement efforts. Let's say that a school improvement plan has the goal of increasing mathematics performance. Important data sources might include curriculum maps or lesson plans to determine a baseline on how much time is spent teaching math. This information can be disaggregated or subdivided by grade level and percentage of teachers trained in the current math program or have specializations in that area and inventories of instructional materials and resources (for example, which textbooks, kits, and other published materials teachers use).

# Visually Effective Data Displays

Well-crafted data displays clarify and communicate often complex or abstract information. For groups exploring data, visually vibrant displays capture and focus attention. As discussed in chapter 2 (page 32), a large data display serves as a third point, physically separating the group from the data and objectifying the

*Well-crafted data displays clarify and communicate often complex or abstract information.*

data—making data a *thing*. As a result, the conversation is about what we (colleagues) notice and think about them (the data). This combination increases the emotional safety needed for group members to poke, prod, and question the data and one another.

In contrast, distributing individual and often cluttered printouts dissolves group cohesion. Participants drop into personal searches, viewing the data from their own vantage points. As a result, group members may be sitting side by side, but lose access to one another's perspectives and experiences. This lack of shared interaction limits shared understanding and collective commitment to action.

Effective data displays should be clear, vibrant, and adequately sized for data groups to share them. A ratio of approximately four to six participants to one large data display works to create a focal point. The small group size increases participation and captures individual energy.

Making a display is not a neutral act. The purposeful consideration and choice of display make different data types more accessible to group work. A particular display shapes the conversation by illuminating relationships in the data set and inviting different kinds of inquiry and analysis.

## Choosing the Visual Representation

Effective collaborative inquiry requires a recasting of raw data or typically used tables and charts into more compelling, clear, and accessible displays. In too many cases, displays in schools and school districts are crowded, unclear, and difficult to read. This problem is exemplified by many state and provincial reports.

Following are six common errors in displaying data.

1. **The display does not illustrate relationships within the data:** For example, using a bar graph to illustrate a trend. To show a trend over time, a line graph would be more effective. Choosing the most effective graphic format facilitates the work of data teams. (See figure 4.2.)

2. **The display range visually skews the values:** For example, plotting performance scores ranging between 35 and 72 percent on a vertical axis of 30 to 80 percent. Plotting the scores on a broader scale from 0 to 100 percent would more accurately reflect results.

3. **The display uses colors with no or low contrast:** For example, using several shades of blue for different subgroups or trend lines. Use contrasting colors for different bars, lines, or pie slices to eliminate visual confusion. Note: Save really bright colors for information that needs to stand out.

4. **The display attempts to squeeze too much information into one chart or graph:** For example, including several subject areas, multiple grade levels, and subgroups in one display. Create several different displays to make the data less overwhelming.

5. **The display labels are difficult to read:** For example, labeling the horizontal (or $x$) axis with vertical type or using a font that is too small is hard to read from a distance. Create labels that are clear and easy to read. Note: Type set on an angle is also ineffective.

6. **The display uses graphic effects without purpose:** For example, overusing 3-D effects. Flashy displays create visual clutter and can actually hide some of the values when bars overlap. Leave the special effects to video games.

### Bar Graphs

Bar graphs can be used to display comparisons, rankings, and change over time, for example, performance in two content areas or performance by subgroup or proficiency levels. Stacked bars show the elements that comprise the total while distinguishing the relative size of the parts, such as stacking proficiency levels within a whole grade level.

Deviation bar graphs display the data above and below a baseline, or the pluses and minuses of an issue or deviations from a standard, such as a locally established benchmark or a nationally referenced norm.

### Pictographs

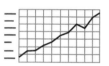

Representing data as pictures makes a creative and eye-catching variation from the more commonly used graphic elements. For example, pictographs can replace the icons on a line graph or can be stacked to form the bars in any form of a bar graph.

### Line Graphs

Line graphs display a sloping line or segments of lines, representing change over time. Thus, they are particularly useful for displaying trends, such as reading scores over a period of years. Line graphs can also display comparisons when several lines are used on the same graph, such as reading scores for several schools or several grade levels over several years.

### Pie Charts

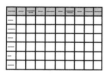

Pie charts display parts of the whole. The size of each part displayed as a percentage makes the relationships among the parts and between the part and whole graphically apparent to observers. For example, pie charts can be used for demographic data, such as teachers' years of experience or students' socioeconomic status.

### Tables

Tables show exact numerical values, such as scores for each student in a class. They are used to portray simple data sets that compare related values, such as scores by teacher by year. Tables are also effective for displaying quantitative information involving more than one unit of measure, such as students by age by performance quartile.

### Scatter Plots

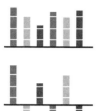

Scatter plots display relationships between two or more variables. They indicate correlations and comparisons, at one point in time or over time, such as scores in reading comprehension and math problem solving.

### Box and Whisker Plots

Box and whisker plots turn raw data into the "shape" of the score distribution, such as standardized test scores, for ease of visual interpretation. The boxes display the distribution of scores, while the whiskers indicate the range above and below the median.

**Figure 4.2: Graphic formats for visual data display.**

*Visual representation is best based on the data's function. . . . The display you choose should be closely related to the question, issue, or topic being explored.*

Visual representation is best based on the data's function. In most cases, data displays are developed from raw data or, more often, data tables. The display you choose should be closely related to the question, issue, or topic being explored. For data sets of twenty numbers or less, tables are more effective than graphs, as they offer more specific information. Tables and charts, including frequency charts, disaggregation tables, and curriculum maps, can be organized as useful displays. Other visuals, such as timelines, schedules, calendars, and other artifacts (student work samples, meeting minutes, sample memos, or newsletters), can also be enlarged to enhance a data display.

Stephen Few (2004) describes four common ways of navigating or interacting with data that inform display choices. Effective displays:

1. Filter out what's not relevant
2. Sort the data to see it in order of magnitude
3. Provide high-level (big picture) and low-level (detailed) views of the data
4. Offer varying views and perspectives of the data using different display types

Well-designed displays reduce the mental effort required to interpret the data, allowing the group to focus on exploring and making meaning from the data.

## • • • • • • • • • Data Story: Using Triangulation • • • • • • • • •

For a full year, New City School District has been implementing a three-pronged plan to improve math performance: a revised curriculum, a new instructional program, and a cohort of building-level math coaches.

At Northside Elementary School, the math coach is leading a vertical team of six teachers through the collaborative learning cycle. They are meeting to generate causal theories and determine additional data to guide their plans.

The coach begins.

> "So, based on our state test, problem solving is jumping out as an issue for all grade levels."

Group members chime in.

> "Well, I know at fourth grade, it's because students don't come with good computational skills, and that takes them off track. So, we need to look at whether that might be an effect across all grade levels."

> "Well, for my kids, it's more about their reading comprehension. They don't know how to read the problem to sort for critical information."

The coach intervenes, with a process suggestion:

> "Before we get too far, let's step back a bit and see what patterns appear in these state data."

The group breaks into pairs and reviews the data displays. It appears that there is not a significant, schoolwide gap in computation skills. Members agree to take a closer look at the issue.

Teachers decide to review the data, class by class and kid by kid, comparing the state math data to the state reading scores for three years. The strongest pattern that emerges across this period of time is the correlation between reading comprehension and problem solving, with gaps in both areas for a large percentage of students. Computation does not seem to be an issue overall.

The coach continues, "Given this additional perspective, what are some causal theories we might pursue?"

> "Well, I think the problem is that kids who aren't strong readers may have computation skills, but can't apply them inside of a word problem. They have difficulty interpreting the question, so they don't know which math operations to use."

> "If that's true, then we would want to look at using math word problems in our reading comprehension lessons to increase their skill in understanding what a problem is asking for."

> "Before we start overhauling our lesson plans, what can we use to confirm that we've nailed the problem? I think we need to get some grade-level and classroom-based data."

> "Yes, we need to see whether the same pattern holds for the assessments built into our new curriculum."

> "We can also script some think-alouds from kids at both ends of the performance range at each grade level."

> "We should also look at which grades and classrooms are getting the best results in this area, so we can learn more about what's going on."

The coach suggests that the group members begin by collecting think-alouds from their own students and recruiting other grade-level teachers to do the same. She will organize the curricular assessments and provide data displays for the next meeting. The coach brings the meeting to a close by charting these agreements and clarifying logistics for the next meeting.

• • • • • • • • • • • • • • • • • • • • • • • • • • • • • • • • • •

# Exercise Your Learning

Use the information from this chapter to do the following:

1. Design a data collection tool that you might use to gather data on an issue you are presently exploring.

2. Complete the Information Altitudes Exercise reproducible using a specific skill set.

3. With samples of your own data, create a visually vibrant display. Consider multiple options, and be prepared to explain your choices.

## Extend Your Learning

Perceptual Edge (www.perceptualedge.com) is a source for learning how to design simple information displays for effective analysis and communication by Stephen Few. Other valuable sources include *Now You See It: Simple Visualization Techniques for Quantitative Analysis* (Few, 2009) and *Show Me the Numbers: Designing Tables and Graphs to Enlighten* (Few, 2004).

Edward Tufte (www.edwardtufte.com/tufte) is a source for increasing the sophistication and visual intelligence of your graphic displays and to learn how to turn data into engaging information. Edward Tufte (1983) is the author of *The Visual Display of Quantitative Information*.

Visit http://marciakastner.com for insights on the impact of poorly designed test questions.

# Information Altitudes Exercise

Think of a specific skill set or knowledge base that you want to explore, such as reading comprehension or math problem solving. Using the following table, identify data sources at each level of information, as indicated.

Area of exploration: _____

| Information Altitudes | Data Source |
| --- | --- |
| International | |
| National | |
| State or Province | |
| District | |
| School, Grade Level, or Department | |
| Classroom | |

# Types of Survey Questions

## Background and Demographic Questions

- Concern the interviewee's identifying characteristics
- Are distinguished by their specific and somewhat routine nature

*Examples: How many years have you been teaching here? What level of education have you completed?*

## Experience and Behavior Questions

- Ask about what a person does or has done
- Elicit descriptions of observable experiences, behaviors, activities, and actions

*Example: If I had been in the classroom with you, what might I have seen or heard?*

## Knowledge Questions

- Designed to find out about the respondent's perspective on empirical data
- Seek factual information such as rules, regulations, program data, logistics, and so on

*Examples: How many planning periods are scheduled each week? How many students are scheduled for special services?*

## Cognitive Questions

- Aimed at understanding the cognitive and interpretive processes of people
- Tell us about people's interpretations, analyses, and inferences

*Example: What do you think about _____?*

## Affective Questions

- Seek to understand people's emotional responses to their experiences
- Will often be responded to with adjectives (such as *happy*, *responsible*, *intimidated*, or *frustrated*)

*Examples: How do you feel about _____? What are your reactions to _____?*

## Sensory Questions

- Ask about what is seen, heard, touched, tasted, and smelled
- Elicit vivid descriptions or events or environments

*Example: When you walk into the classroom, what do you see?*

## Identity and Value Questions

- Seek expressions of identity, values, and beliefs
- Tell us about interviewee's goals, intentions, desires, and values

  *Examples: What do you value most about* _____*? What would you most like to see happen?*

## Role Play and Simulations

- Provide a context for potentially difficult questions
- Put the interviewee in the stance of expert
- Reduce the personal nature of some questions

  *Examples: Suppose I just started teaching here, what would be the most important things I would need to know to be successful? Suppose you needed to get something done around here, what would you do?*

# CHAPTER FIVE

# Developing High-Performing Groups

Grappling with worthy problems requires a set of knowledge, skills, and dispositions, both for group members and for the group itself. Groups flounder when their problems are bigger than their skill sets; they need protocols, structures, and skills to define messy problems in ways they can pursue productively.

In chapter 1, we described seven actions of high-performing groups (see page 11).

1. Maintain a clear focus.
2. Embrace a spirit of inquiry.
3. Put data at the center.
4. Honor commitments to learners and learning.
5. Cultivate relational trust.
6. Seek equity.
7. Assume collective responsibility.

Groups express these qualities when individuals develop and apply essential understandings and skills to their work. A cohesive, high-performing group attends to relationships while engaging in its tasks. How group members relate to one another and to their work grow out of the ways in which individuals communicate with one another, regard and empathize with one another, and connect the ideas they generate with their personal and collective work.

> *A cohesive, high-performing group attends to relationships while engaging in its tasks.*

## Group Member Knowledge and Skill

Navigating the currents of collaborative work both requires and enhances knowledge of self and others and knowledge of what makes groups effective (Lipton & Wellman, 2011b). High levels of consciousness regarding these knowledge bases inform group members' choices in the moment and over time, creating a greater degree of productivity, satisfaction, and group growth. The following descriptions capture the essential knowledge and skill base necessary for effective data-driven collaboration and for developing high-performing groups.

## Knowledge of Self and Others

Group members vary in their comfort and skills when working with data. The deep data work described in chapter 4 requires technical knowledge of specific types of data and displays, observational and interpretive skills, and most importantly, analytical skills. Content-area knowledge and assessment literacy also come into play. Group members need to know their own and others' capabilities in these arenas and respect requests for clarification. Ensuring shared understandings is an important goal for high-performing data teams.

When data-shy group members avoid the discomfort of not knowing or not feeling competent, they may defer to the perceived experts in the group. It is important to remember that expertise and confidence are not the same. Unequal access to knowledge creates power imbalances in groups. Over time, these asymmetries create divisions or hierarchies within the group, reducing both cohesion and effectiveness.

More knowledgeable group members face related challenges. Their impulse and ego control matter greatly to the group's ultimate development. When experts dominate a group's work, their own enthusiasm hinders the engagement and learning of their colleagues. Relational trust is necessary for and also develops from the mutual learning of balanced data explorations.

## Knowledge of Values, Beliefs, and Assumptions About Learners and Learning

All group members bring distinct worldviews to their personal and collective work. These values, beliefs, and assumptions about learners and learning apply to both students and colleagues. They derive from individual experience, shaping the interpretation of data, the generation of causal theories, and the development of solutions. Being aware of similarities and differences in underlying perspectives helps us understand what we might notice or miss in the data and the meaning we might make from it.

Groups and group members suffer from belief blindness when they narrow the scope of their explorations and interpretations by seeing only what they expect to see or use data as evidence to support their beliefs. In addition, group work stalls or is distorted when the viewpoints are too inclusive and there are no criteria for sorting perspectives that align with established student and group member learning goals from those that do not. Seeking equity is necessary for and also develops when appreciation for diverse ways of processing is central to nonjudgmental data explorations. For example, well-structured team protocols that include members with different roles, years of experience, content expertise, and work-style preferences support this approach.

## Knowledge of Work-Style Preferences

Four tensions are classic in all groups: (1) task–relationship, (2) certainty–ambiguity, (3) detail–big picture, and (4) autonomy–collaboration (Lipton & Wellman, 2011b). These differences present as continuums, not fixed points. Working with data amplifies these preferences, shaping the underlying dynamic of the group. The four tensions are:

> **Task–relationship:** *Values about how time should be used, the press for efficient work completion, and the need for all voices to be heard produce tensions in groups. Differing preferences for attention to task and patience with process cause friction and limit productivity.*

> **Certainty–ambiguity:** *Individual group members vary dramatically in their need for surety in the data interpretation before moving forward with plans of action. Comfort with some degree of ambiguity is essential for moving the work forward. This polarity can freeze a group's progress.*

> **Detail–big picture:** *A focus on the specifics of data is a source of comfort for some group members; for others, a broader view energizes their thinking. While each of these preferences adds value to group work, tensions emerge when these work styles conflict.*

> **Autonomy–collaboration:** *The energy demands for working in data teams vary dramatically for individual group members. Individuals are often either drained or energized by collaborative work. Awareness of these preferences helps group members understand each other and frame the work accordingly. (p. 9)*

Work-style preferences are sources of comfort and discomfort related to work with data. These preferences can lead to task, decision, or conflict avoidance, which can undermine the collaborative potential. To meet the demands of data work, group members need to be emotionally resourceful, honoring style differences, flexing across personal preferences, and showing the deep commitment to learners and learning is necessary for and develops from thoughtfully structured group work. (See the Four Dynamical Tensions reproducibles, pages 88–90, to assess your group work. Visit **go.solution-tree.com/teams** to download the reproducibles in this book.)

## Knowledge of Effective Groups: Stages of Group Development

Group development occurs in stages. Spending time together does not produce growth. Along the novice to expert continuum, there are well-established groups still functioning at the beginning stages. When members share a common developmental map and agree on performance descriptors, they can assess, reflect, set goals, and improve. Groups need to anticipate that development might be uneven, with some regression under certain conditions—for example, the addition of new members, changes in leadership, or controversial tasks. The challenges of working with data and making it central to the conversations have the potential to cause a reversion to earlier developmental functioning. This possibility increases the importance of a group's conscious and conscientious attention to its own development.

Tuckman (1965) describes four stages of group development: forming, storming, norming, and performing. Each stage blends two aspects: (1) task-related behavior and (2) interpersonal behavior.

1. **Forming:** The key word here is *safety*. As members familiarize themselves with each other and the task at hand, the data exploration is often cursory. The conversation surface stays smooth as group members avoid uncomfortable topics and difficult questions. Group members at this stage remain dependent on leaders for direction, permission, and protection. To move forward as a group, members must be willing to deal with discomfort—their own and others'.

2. **Storming:** The key word here is *resistance*. Confronting the demands of group processes and task requirements stimulates self-protective mechanisms. Turbulent conversations occur as group members transition from *me* to *us*: conflicting about data, leadership, task design, rules, and responsibilities. Participation is uneven as some members attempt to dominate while others withdraw. To move forward as a group, members must be willing to be as invested in the ideas of others as they are in their own.

3. **Norming:** The key word here is *openness*. As relational trust and task confidence increase, group members welcome diverse perspectives, actively inquire, and share leadership. Waves of new ideas stimulate conversation flow. There is an identity shift: members see themselves as part of an effective group, resulting in shared information, resources, and feedback. To move forward as a group, members must be willing to grow, setting new and challenging goals for themselves as learners.

4. **Performing:** The key word here is *flexibility*. Group members skillfully adjust to the dynamics of deeper data work, attending to the emotional and cognitive needs of colleagues. Conversations involve a rich crosscurrent of ideas. There are high degrees of relational trust and collective responsibility for the success of the work. Within this stage, there is a healthy balance between self-focus and group focus; group members are able to appropriately self-assert or integrate. Skillful and systematic experimentation and problem solving are energy sources.

The primary challenge to group development is the transition in identity from individual practitioner to member of a high-performing group. This shift requires that members see themselves as part of the group and believe there is mutual investment in its success. In essence, Tuckman's (1965) stages describe this journey. In contrast with the original work, we suggest that the progression is recursive, not linear, based on Smith (2005; see figure 5.1). After forming, groups often cycle between the other three stages as topics, contexts, membership, and other conditions shift. For example, a group that has been functioning consistently in the performing stage might be derailed by a volatile or controversial topic and might need to cycle back to norming then storming before being able to function with its previous skill level.

> *The primary challenge to group development is the transition in identity from individual practitioner to member of a high-performing group.*

Such topics include using standards-based grading, creating common assessments, and increasing diversity in advanced placement classes.

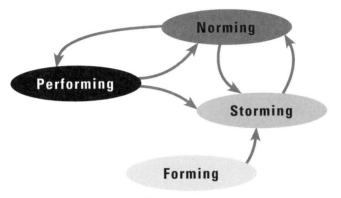

Source: *Adapted from Smith, 2005. Used with permission.*

**Figure 5.1: Nonlinear stages of group development.**

Another challenge to group development is overcoming fear of conflict. This emotional resourcefulness requires that group members confront their own discomfort and have tools for separating interpersonal from cognitive conflict. The development of these capacities is a fundamental aspect of transitioning between stages.

Oversimplification of this or any developmental model occurs when groups lack clear descriptors, shared understanding, and tools for assessing their own growth.

## *Knowledge of Process and Structures*

*Know how to structure group work.* Groups that develop and apply a shared repertoire of process strategies work more productively and efficiently than those that do not. Purposefully structured interactions shape the quality of group members' experience and produce individual and collective learning. Well-designed work sessions scaffold interaction patterns and thinking processes. (See Group Work Structures, page 92.)

When working with data, consider group size and composition. Periodically creating small task groups of two to four increases safety, focus, and participation. Choices about materials and displays are also critical. Shared data displays focus a group; individual data sets create disintegration. Other structural elements include public charts, recording sheets, public timers, and group roles.

*Know when to structure group work.* While structuring choices are always important considerations, they are essential under certain conditions (such as when group skills are not well developed, there are high levels of stress or fatigue, the task is complex or controversial, or there is high pressure for immediate results). One hallmark of high-performing groups is recognition of these conditions, whether in anticipation of group work or during it. In these circumstances, a skillful group will elect to impose increased structure on their own process.

# Skills for Talking About Data

When working with data, how groups talk is as important as what they talk about. In addition to a firm knowledge base, a set of verbal and nonverbal skills is needed to move groups and their work forward. Groups develop as the quality and skill of their conversations develop.

The following are tools for talking:

- Listen without judgment.

- Pause to create space for thinking.

- Paraphrase to support relationships, increase understanding, and mediate thinking.

- Inquire to focus and open thinking.

## Listen Without Judgment

Listening is about relationships. It involves a psychological connection with the speaker. To listen nonjudgmentally requires internal discipline and valuing what others have to say. In group work with data, listening requires more than waiting for a turn to talk. Skilled listeners attend to the message behind the words with a desire to understand frames of reference, underlying emotions, and assumptions. Group members also listen for omissions, biases, and gaps in logic or information related to the data. Fluency with this fundamental skill includes qualities of listening during particular modes of discourse. For example, we listen for connections during dialogue and for distinctions during discussions. (See chapter 6, page 95.)

> *Listening is about relationships. It involves a psychological connection with the speaker.*

## Pause to Create Space for Thinking

There is a powerful connection between pausing and the quality of thinking during work sessions. Conversational pace affects both the emotional and intellectual climate for group members. Fast-paced interactions may exclude more introspective members. Skillful groups realize that complex thinking takes time (Wellman & Lipton, 2004).

There are four functions for pausing during group work.

1. **Pausing after speaking or asking a question:** These pauses presuppose readiness, willingness, and capacity for thought and reflection.

2. **Pausing after group member responses:** These pauses provide time for the initial respondent to take in, reflect on, and retrieve additional information. They also offer opportunities for *daisy chains*, or related contributions from other group members.

3. **Pausing before paraphrasing, asking a question, responding, or offering ideas:** These pauses protect a speaker's need to craft thoughtful language, model the importance of thinking before speaking, and display a value for thoughtfulness.

4. **Pausing collectively throughout a work session:** These group pauses pace the conversation for inclusion of all members. They provide time for group observation, summarization, and reflection.

Discomfort with pausing keeps groups from becoming skillful. Two misconceptions prevail. One is the mistaken correlation between speed and intelligence—the faster I respond, the more I know. The other involves perspectives about the use of time. Pausing requires going slow to ultimately accelerate group development and improve the quality of collaborative work.

## Paraphrase to Support Relationships, Increase Understanding, and Mediate Thinking

Thoughtfully designed paraphrases foster relationships by reducing the gaps between group members, communicating a sense of regard and a desire to understand. At a basic level, paraphrasing means listening for and reflecting on a colleague's thoughts and emotions. In groups, the paraphrase honors contributions, links ideas, and establishes a platform for further thought.

Four functions for paraphrase follow. See table 5.1 (page 82) for examples.

1. **Paraphrase to acknowledge and clarify:** This paraphrase form restates the essence of statements and provides opportunities to calibrate a speaker's content and emotions.

2. **Paraphrase to summarize and organize:** This paraphrase form offers themes and categories to create containers, compare, sequence, or otherwise organize initiating statements. This type of paraphrase is especially useful when there have been multiple contributions and a large volume of information shared.

3. **Paraphrase to shift the level of abstraction up:** This paraphrase form moves language and thinking to higher conceptual levels, illuminating large ideas or increasing precision and focus. Skillful application of this paraphrase form requires listening for embedded values, beliefs, and assumptions and offering categorical labels (higher conceptual levels).

Shifting up is particularly effective in goal setting, problem framing, and problem-solving situations. The abstract labels widen the potential solution set and encourage a broader exploration of ideas and strategies.

4.  **Paraphrase to shift the level of abstraction down:** This paraphrase form moves language and thinking to lower conceptual levels. Shifting down is especially effective in data work for clarifying communication, calibrating standards, and increasing precision of thought. Skillful application requires the paraphraser to provide examples and nonexamples (lower levels of abstraction) to calibrate and mediate thinking. For example, the speaker might say, "This assessment shows really poor performance in fourth-grade writing." To which the responder might paraphrase, "So, they have vocabulary skills, but they're not yet proficient with main idea and transitions."

**Table 5.1: Four Paraphrase Functions**

| Acknowledging and Clarifying | | |
|---|---|---|
| | **A Group Member Might Say** | **Possible Paraphrase** |
| **Content** | "It's clear the kids weren't ready for this test." | "You're concerned about preparing students for success." |
| **Emotions** | "These displays are so confusing. I don't understand them." | "These data seem overwhelming at this point." |
| **Summarizing and Organizing** | | |
| | **A Group Member Might Say** | **Possible Paraphrase** |
| **Containers** | "I'm really dismayed. The data seem to indicate that in language arts, the students are completing their assignments and working both independently and interdependently to build comprehension skills. But in our math classes, the same students are unfocused and off task so much of the time that we can't even give them independent work." | "So, you're exploring two distinct data sets: language arts and math." |
| **Comparisons and Contrasts** | "The incoming freshmen seem so much more ready this year. They have most of the basic skills they'll need for succeeding in higher-level math classes." | "As you compare this year's ninth grade to previous years, you're anticipating greater readiness and better performance." |
| **Sequences** | "There is a ton of work to do here. We need to organize the data displays, schedule meeting times and places, and then get inside the data to determine patterns of errors, what might be causing them, and what we can do." | "So, you're proposing four tasks. First we need to nail down the logistics, then we can examine data to look for error patterns, then consider causes, and finally craft intervention plans." |

| Shifting the Level of Abstraction Up | | |
|---|---|---|
| | **A Group Member Might Say** | **Possible Paraphrase** |
| **Goal** | "These students really can't handle the textbook. It is over their heads conceptually and very thick in text with few tables or illustrations to guide understanding." | "So, your goal is to find instructional materials that will meet your students' needs." |
| **Value** | "These test data are too limited and too far from my everyday classroom instruction. By the time I get the results, I'm teaching entirely different units and skills." | "So, it's important to you to have timely, student-centered feedback to guide instruction." |
| Shifting the Level of Abstraction Down | | |
| | **A Group Member Might Say** | **Possible Paraphrase** |
| **Example** | "These students really can't handle the textbook. It is over their heads conceptually and very thick in text with few tables or illustrations to guide understanding." | "So, you're concerned about the format and reading level of the book being too challenging for your students." |
| **Nonexample** | "These test data are too limited and too far from my everyday classroom instruction. By the time I get the results, I'm teaching entirely different units and skills." | "So, you're not concerned about using the assessment data to inform your planning, you're concerned about receiving the data at an efficient time." |

Although the paraphrase is a powerful response choice, it is often underused because of negative experiences or lack of skill. Discomfort with paraphrase limits a group member's ability to build relationships and build on the ideas of others. This avoidance comes from several sources. Paraphrase has often been taught or experienced as a simplistic verbal response, creating an echo or parrot phrase; it can feel artificial or mechanical, as in the pattern of using the personal pronoun to begin ("I think I hear you saying . . ."). This annoying habit makes paraphrase a ritualized reflex, checked off so responders can now take the conversation in their own preferred direction. Another difficulty is that though paraphrase has been taught as a verbal skill, it is ultimately an *auditory* discipline. Skillful paraphrase requires listening deeply to the story beneath the story and suspending the impulse to control the conversation.

## Inquire to Focus and Open Thinking

Inquiry joins pausing and paraphrasing to engage, energize, and organize thoughtful group work with data. Effective inquiry has two key characteristics: (1) there is an implied or explicit thinking process to the question, and (2) there are no preconceived or preferred responses.

As figure 5.2 illustrates, there are two primary ways a group might inquire into a data set: inquire to open thinking or inquire to focus thinking.

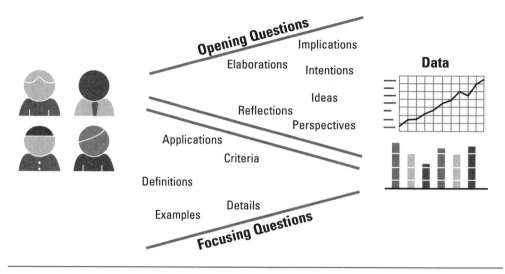

**Figure 5.2: Opening and focusing questions.**

1. **Inquiry to open thinking:** Questions that open thinking expand and deepen ideas, perspectives, and breadth by inquiring for implications, intentions, elaborations, perspectives, new or additional ideas, and reflections.

2. **Inquiry to focus thinking:** Questions that focus thinking increase precision of language and thought by inquiring for details, examples, applications, definitions, and criteria.

Discomfort with inquiry often emerges from a fear of challenging colleagues' thoughts, actions, or choices. Without syntactical and intonational skillfulness, questioning can feel like interrogation. As a result, colleagues may perceive questions as challenges to debate, resulting in a right and wrong dynamic. Schwarz (2002) makes a distinction between genuine and rhetorical inquiry. Inquiry with the intention of learning is very different than asking a question that has a preferred response by leading with "Have you thought of . . . ?" or "Have you tried . . . ?"

Questions that support learning open thought, create new possibilities, and have no right answers. Examples include "What are some options we might consider here?" or "What are some other perspectives we might be missing?"

Table 5.2 offers several syntactical substitutions that invite thinking by creating conditions of psychological safety. The terms on the left tend to limit thinking and promote defensiveness by communicating that there is a preferred correct response. The substitutions on the right encourage risk taking by communicating that there are multiple possible responses.

**Table 5.2: Syntactical Substitutions for Terms That Limit Thinking**

| Terms That Limit Thinking | Syntactical Substitutions | Examples |
|---|---|---|
| The | Some | Instead of asking, "What is *the* reason for this learning gap?" try asking, "What are *some* reasons for this learning gap?" |
| Could | Might | Instead of asking, "How *could* you improve this rubric?" try asking, "How *might* you improve this rubric?" |
| Is | Seems | Instead of asking, "What *is* the cause of student success with this concept?" try asking, "What *seems* to be the cause of student success with this concept?" |
| Why | What | Instead of asking, "*Why* do our students struggle with writing clearly?" try asking, "*What* are some of the reasons our students struggle with writing clearly?" |

# Methods for Assessing Growth

Groups and group members develop when they purposefully use data about their own performance to set, monitor, and assess goals. Group members monitor themselves to increase awareness about their own choices, actions, and influence. Groups monitor collectively for the same purposes. As described in this chapter, group members pay attention to a variety of internal and external elements to determine their knowledge and skill levels and their own group development.

Formative instruments, including rubrics, surveys, inventories, exit slips, stem completions, and inquiry logs, are readily available. What is important is that groups select and consistently apply tools that align with their beliefs and aspirations. In addition to having the tools for measuring growth, groups need to preserve time for structured and systematic reflection about the data these instruments generate.

Enhanced group member skills emerge from well-structured interactions. A group's shared repertoire of structures and degree of skill influence group members' choices; they are the means by which colleagues organize their interaction patterns and focus on their work. Development accelerates when a cycle of goal setting, monitoring, and reflecting is an integral part of a group's work.

*Enhanced group member skills emerge from well-structured interactions. A group's shared repertoire of structures and degree of skill influence group members' choices.*

• • • • • **Data Story: Moving From Storming to Norming** • • • • •

It is the first meeting after the winter break for the data team at Atlantic Middle School. Before immersing themselves in a new round of student data cycles, group members agreed that it was a good time to review their own growth as a team. Before leaving for break, the group completed a Stages of Group Development inventory, which is now the focus of the conversation.

"Given the scoring on individual inventories, it's pretty clear that most of us believe we are not yet through the storming stage."

"Yeah, we still seem to have some strong feelings and opinions about whose way is the best way."

"And when those opinions are conflicting, we don't always give others a chance to voice their thinking."

"So, what do we need to do to move past this stage?"

"Let's take a look at the indicators on this inventory and see what we're missing."

"It's pretty clear that we don't use shared standards to help us resolve conflicts. It's a bit ironic that as a data team, we use standards for students, but don't apply any to our own group work."

"Most of the time, we also talk over each other, and we don't really listen before advocating for our own ideas."

"So, what are some next steps?"

"You mean, what would each of us need to do, and what would all of us need to do?"

"Well, for one thing, we could give each other the benefit of the doubt and remember that we really do all care about what's best for kids."

"Yeah, we really need to trust each other more—and maybe that would come from agreeing to try out some new ideas or some things that might be a little uncomfortable at first."

"We also could use some structures or protocols to make sure everyone has a chance to talk."

"I'll be honest here. I'm really impatient and tend to either interrupt or just mentally vacate the room. I need to take the time to understand where others are coming from before judging. I know that's going to be a challenge."

"So, what are we willing to agree to?"

"And how should we prioritize next steps?"

"Well, for one thing, we need to be sure to get lots of ideas, preferably different ideas on the table before making any judgments or narrowing our choices."

"And each of us needs to agree to listen, not interrupt, pause before jumping in, and spend more time asking questions about others' ideas than rejecting them out of hand."

"Well, then, I still think we need some protocols to structure that. Some for generating ideas, some for ensuring individual and group think time, and maybe some for formal inquiry into ideas."

"OK, then how about we take turns creating and facilitating a process agenda and save time at the beginning of each meeting to remind ourselves and at the end to assess how we did. The facilitator can be responsible for documenting that as part of the process."

"That sounds like a plan. Let's draw names out of this basket to set up the leadership schedule."

. . . . . . . . . . . . . . . . . . . . . . . . . . . . . . . . . . . . .

# Exercise Your Learning

Complete the Stages of Group Development inventory (page 91) to assess how the stages of group development apply to a group with whom you are presently working. (Visit **go.solution-tree.com/teams** for the online-only scoring rubric "Determining Your Stage of Group Development.") Use the results from the inventory to structure a data-driven dialogue and to set goals for continued learning. To focus the interaction, make a public display on which to record responses.

Consider the following options for application of the Stages of Group Development.

- Ask individual group members to complete the inventory, then compare responses as a group.

- Subdivide the group into pairs or trios to complete the inventory.

- Complete the inventory as a full group with public recording.

Note: In each case, be sure to generate specific examples to support the scaled responses. Use the Group Work Structures reproducible (page 92, or visit **go.solution-tree.com/teams**) to purposefully structure interactions that shape the quality of group members' experience and produce individual and collective learning.

# Extend Your Learning

Workshop Exercises (www.workshopexercises.com) offers a variety of resources, exercises, and inventories for developing groups and their leaders. Within the toolkit are forms that can be used as they are or can be easily modified to fit local contexts.

Group Development Tools Practitioners Can Use (Minahan & Hutton, 2002) is a downloadable and accessible overview of the group development models of Wilfred Bion and William Schutz (www.ntl.org/upload/Group DevelopmentTools.pdf). It helps analyze the stages of group development and supports meeting design work to match and stretch group members' needs and responsiveness.

# Four Dynamical Tensions: Assessing Your Group Membership

Under stress we tend to revert to our underlying preferences. Fatigue, overload, project and decision deadlines, internal and external social and political pressures, and controversial topics are some of the possible sources of tension that we might experience during group work. Imagine yourself in such a setting as you work in a particular group. Place a check mark on your likely default positions in such a situation.

Task _____ | _____ | _____ | _____ Relationship

Certainty _____ | _____ | _____ | _____ Ambiguity

Detail _____ | _____ | _____ | _____ Big Picture

Autonomy _____ | _____ | _____ | _____ Collaboration

The learning journey is always a quest for increasing flexibility to produce more options for ourselves and our groups. Reflect on the following questions, and record your thoughts.

What are some patterns of discomfort to monitor in yourself as a group member?

_____

_____

_____

_____

_____

What are some hot-button topics coming up in your groups that will require personal flexibility for you to be a more influential group member?

_____

_____

_____

_____

_____

# Four Dynamical Tensions: Assessing Your Leadership

How we behave as a group leader is not always the same as how we behave as a group member. Under stress we tend to revert to our underlying preferences. Fatigue, overload, project and decision deadlines, internal and external social and political pressures, and controversial topics are some of the possible sources of tension that we might experience during group work. Imagine yourself in such a setting as you work with a particular group as the leader. Place a check mark on your likely default positions in such a situation.

Task _____ | _____ | _____ | _____ Relationship

Certainty _____ | _____ | _____ | _____ Ambiguity

Detail _____ | _____ | _____ | _____ Big Picture

Autonomy _____ | _____ | _____ | _____ Collaboration

The learning journey is always a quest for increasing flexibility to produce more options for ourselves and our groups. Reflect on the following questions, and record your thoughts.

What are some patterns of discomfort to monitor in yourself as a group leader?

_____

_____

_____

_____

_____

What are some hot-button topics coming up in groups you lead that will require personal flexibility for you as a leader?

_____

_____

_____

_____

_____

# Four Dynamical Tensions: Assessing Your Group

Under stress group members tend to revert to their underlying preferences. Groups ultimately develop working styles based on the personalities of individual members melding into a social contract that defines tacit agreements about how the group should operate, especially under duress. Fatigue, overload, project and decision deadlines, internal and external social and political pressures, and controversial topics are some of the possible sources of tension that groups might be experiencing. Think about a group you are presently leading; consider how this group typically reacts under stress. Place a check mark on the likely default positions in these situations.

Task _____ | _____ | _____ | _____ Relationship

Certainty _____ | _____ | _____ | _____ Ambiguity

Detail _____ | _____ | _____ | _____ Big Picture

Autonomy _____ | _____ | _____ | _____ Collaboration

For group leaders, detecting patterns and anticipating group dynamics are important design and delivery skills. Reflect on the following questions, and record your thoughts as you plan for upcoming sessions with this group.

What are some patterns you anticipate that will inform your design and delivery choices?

_____

_____

_____

_____

_____

What structures and strategies might you apply to manage the discomforts that may arise as group members engage with their tasks?

_____

_____

_____

_____

_____

# Stages of Group Development

Assess how the stages of group development (forming, storming, norming, and performing) relate to your group's tasks and relationships.

| Task: Rate patterns of interaction as they relate to the work at hand. | Scale: 1–4 (Forming to Performing) | Relationship: Rate interpersonal dynamics. | Scale: 1–4 (Forming to Performing) |
|---|---|---|---|
| Our team has a clear purpose that each member can describe accurately. | | Our team has agreed on process norms. | |
| Our team has clear goals that relate to our task. | | Team members honor our process norms. | |
| Team members can clearly explain ways that our tasks contribute to the mission and vision of our organization. | | Our team has strategies for addressing personal discomfort. | |
| Our team sets goals for our own team development. | | Our team has strategies for addressing group discomfort. | |
| Our team routinely takes time to monitor our progress toward team goals. | | Team members productively express disagreement. | |
| Our team has and applies clear criteria for task success. | | Team members acknowledge and address power struggles. | |
| Our team has clear decision-making processes that each member understands and applies. | | Team members resolve conflicts productively. | |
| Team members evenly distribute task responsibility. | | Team members share leadership. | |
| Team members efficiently access and utilize resources to achieve our task. | | Team members balance contributions without individuals dominating. | |
| Team members agree on priorities. | | Team members balance advocacy for their own ideas with inquiry into the ideas of others. | |
| Team members use shared protocols to move the work forward. | | Team members seek others' perspectives. | |
| Team members assess their work for inclusion of different perspectives before finalizing a task. | | Team members appreciate and honor differences. | |
| Team members search for resources outside of their current knowledge base. | | Team members self-monitor to determine when and how to participate productively. | |
| Team members are willing to take responsibility for all aspects of the work. | | Team members trust one another to follow through on commitments. | |
| Team members actively seek new challenges to continuous improvement. | | Team members balance assertion for their own needs with attention to others' needs and preferences. | |

# Group Work Structures

Purposefully structured interactions shape the quality of group members' experience and produce individual and collective learning. These thoughtful design choices influence both group development and task success. Satisfying sessions require an exchange of viewpoints in which group members listen to understand others' feelings and opportunities to influence the final results. Well-engineered work sessions produce these outcomes.

The following elements can be inserted into many of the strategies described in this book. These components can be mixed and matched to amplify the effectiveness of a strategy by shaping interaction or explicit thinking processes.

## Interaction Structures

In many groups, balancing participation is a challenge. Breaking the group into smaller parts, such as pairs or trios, or providing structures that require a response sequence increases the likelihood that all members will have a voice and a chance to be heard.

**Brainstorm and Pass** is a structure for balancing participation by having participants brainstorm in sequence. The intention of this structure is to support rapid, nonjudgmental generation of ideas.

*Directions:* One participant begins by offering an idea related to the topic. Additional items are added using a round-robin pattern (see page 2 of this reproducible): one idea at a time, one participant at a time in sequence. To maintain fluidity, group members can "pass," but are still included in subsequent rounds. Note: The recorder also gets a turn in each rotation.

**Pairs Squared** is a structure for expanding a partnered conversation to a larger group in order to extend ideas, connections, and perspectives. Depending on the tasks at hand, pairs can be intentionally organized and composed of role-alike or cross-role colleagues (same or different grade levels or content areas), different years of experiences, or even philosophical approaches to teaching. Pairs can also be randomly chosen or based on group-member choice.

*Directions:* After pairs have been established and completed some aspect of a strategy, invite each pair to join another pair to form quartets. Note: This can be modified to joining three pairs together, Pairs Times Three.

**Partner's Report** is a structure for listening to and sharing others' ideas. This approach produces respectful attention to people's ideas. The structure promotes new voices sharing examples, builds the collective knowledge base, and creates a fuller community. It's also an opportunity to check for participants' current understanding.

*Directions:* Individuals generate an idea, recollection, connection, key point, or so on and then share it with a partner. Partners listen to each other and prepare to share their colleague's ideas, not their own. The group leader establishes a sequence or process for sharing with the full group.

page 1 of 2

**Round-Robin** is a structure for balancing participation and providing a space for everyone's contribution by establishing a sequence for sharing.

*Directions:* Designate a group member to begin sharing to the right; remaining group members contribute in sequence. Note: One choice point is whether or not each contribution is intended to stimulate conversation or if ideas are offered with no cross-talk.

**Walkabouts** provide an opportunity for task groups to view the ideas and work products of others, such as a table or wall-chart display. This interaction pattern widens the knowledge base and provides a shift in cognitive and physical energy.

*Directions:* Establish a time frame and focus for task groups to rotate or move about viewing the work products of other groups. Encourage group members to look for and collect ideas that will stimulate or enhance their own task-group work.

## Thinking Structures

The hectic pace of life in schools travels into the meeting room. For teams to take the time to think often requires specific structuring. The following options are designed to prompt and promote more thoughtful meetings and work sessions.

**10–2** is a structure for stimulating attention and retention by providing intermittent breaks for interaction (Rowe, 1986). These brief talk times occur after approximately ten minutes of input.

*Directions:* Establish partners, and offer a prompt for them to discuss during a pause in a presentation. These might include a brief summary, an application, a key point, or a question.

**From the Balcony** is a structure for shifting perspective to a macro, or bird's-eye, view of a situation or event. This view can be applied to past, present, or future situations.

*Directions:* Direct group members to envision or reflect on some situation or action, such as an effective lesson, a productive meeting, or a parent conference. Have them discuss what they might see and hear from an elevated vantage point. Note: You can organize these observations as a T-chart.

**Stem Completion** is a structure for jumpstarting thoughts and subsequent conversations. This versatile structure can be used before talking with a partner, small group, or full group and after group talk to integrate new thinking.

*Directions:* Offer a visual prompt on a slide screen, chart, or worksheet. Ask individuals to complete the stem. For example, before sharing, ask group members to complete statements such as, "One thing I'm looking forward to during this meeting is," or "One thing I noticed about my students this week is _____." After shared exploration, ask group members to complete statements such as, "One new idea I will apply is _____," or "One goal for my own learning is _____."

# CHAPTER SIX

# *Moving From Dialogue to Discussion to Decision Making*

Talking together is the most fundamental process for groups. Talking and thinking intertwine to produce a group's working culture. How group members talk influences personal and collective thinking. How group members think influences personal and collective talking. By choosing specific ways of interacting when working with data, skillful groups increase the power, productivity, and payoffs of their time together.

> *By choosing specific ways of interacting when working with data, skillful groups increase the power, productivity, and payoffs of their time together.*

While there are multiple forms of discourse, three specific modes are essential when working with data: dialogue, discussion, and decision making. Across these modes, the group's discourse begins with divergent thinking and ultimately converges on one idea (see figure 6.1, page 96). The characteristics of the three modes of discourse are the following.

1. **Dialogue promotes a spirit of shared inquiry within a group:** The intention is to surface multiple perspectives, encourage connection making between ideas and people, and develop shared understandings of these perspectives and ideas. With dialogue, there is no need to influence or agree.

2. **Discussion breaks issues and problems into components and parts:** The intention is to generate and analyze ideas, clarify the distinctions between these ideas, and define success criteria. With discussion, group members critique and advocate, sort and prioritize.

3. **Decision making is choice making:** The intention is to weigh options against success criteria, select the most viable outcome, and set the scene for action planning. With decision making, the group commits to one choice.

These purposeful processes help group members navigate the mental and emotional challenges embedded in data work related to their own teaching

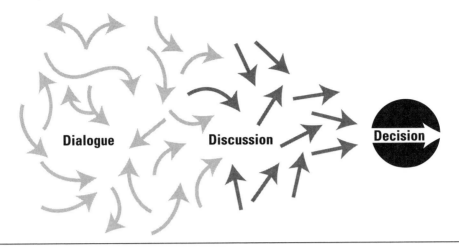

**Figure 6.1: Three modes of discourse—Divergent to convergent thinking.**

practices. Intentionally structured conversations develop richer understandings, a wider range of options, and greater commitment to proposed actions than the typical meeting free-for-all.

The processes of dialogue, discussion, and decision making are sequenced in the collaborative learning cycle described in chapter 2. The embedded questions and spirit of organized curiosity in the activating and engaging phase prepare groups for the rich opportunities of productive dialogue. This spirit extends into the exploring and discovering phase as group members engage with the data before them. The organizing and integrating phase is a transitional point in the cycle. This phase opens with dialogue as group members generate multiple causal theories and then segues into more formal discussion as group members narrow their search to the most likely contributory factors. As they clarify these elements, their discussion moves to decision, resulting in formal commitments to desired outcomes.

Each mode of discourse requires structure and facility with a repertoire of tools for talking. Without knowledge of discourse processes and skills with these tools, group members often default to patterns of advocacy for their own ideas with little exploration of others' ideas. While some participants thrive in the hot zone of debate, others pull back and withdraw from the interaction. Their ideas are lost to the group. Poor process leads to poor decisions; poor decisions lead to weak actions; and weak actions sustain or amplify the problems that initially brought the group to the table. In well-structured group work, members are clear about the process and their roles and responsibilities in it. As a result, the discourse produces task success and growth for the group.

## Three Constraints to Productive Discourse

Irving Janis (1989) identifies three types of group constraints: (1) cognitive constraints, (2) affiliative constraints, and (3) egocentric constraints. While his original research focuses solely on decision making, these factors are at work in most group processes. These constraints limit group members' capacities for effective interaction as they engage in dialogue, discussion, and decision making.

## Cognitive Constraints

Groups hit the cognitive wall when they have limited information about or limited expertise with an issue. For example, this constraint affects groups making high-stakes decisions such as major curriculum or instructional changes based on insufficient data. When problem complexity bumps up against time limitations, groups attempt to simplify the problem by creating small worlds to hold more cognitively manageable formulations. Nobel laureate Herbert Simon, in his work on group decision making, refers to these constructions as *bounded rationality* (as cited in Beach, 1997). These *bounded* representations of the problem are then based on existing information sources so the group can make a rational decision from this limited data set. This tendency leads many groups to seek precedents and look to past practices and solutions for answers to current problems.

Simon also coined the term *satisficing* to describe another way that groups attempt to reduce the demands of information processing (Beach, 1997). They do so by pouncing on the first solution to the bounded problem definition that meets some minimal standards for success that the group has either intentionally or tacitly established. These minimally satisfactory and minimally sufficient solutions allow the group to complete its task without the angst and effort of deeper processing. For example, some schools rush to develop remedial programs to address low performance before examining core instructional practices or other factors that might be producing learning gaps.

## Affiliative Constraints

Group members continually navigate task and relationship tensions. For some group members, the need to belong inhibits their willingness to ask probing questions, put ideas on the table, or offer solutions that may run counter to their colleagues' preferred approaches. Preserving group harmony then leads to shallow conversations, a focus on side issues, and poorly framed decisions. This occurs especially when group members are reluctant to share observations about a data set or speak up when they sense that the group is moving down an unwise path. Avoiding difficult topics amplifies when there is group pressure to achieve consensus.

Groups that overemphasize individual needs for inclusion or spend excessive energy attempting to mollify disgruntled members during dialogue and discussion may be operating within affiliative constraints. These patterns are typical of Tuckman's (1965) forming stage of group development and lead to sloppy decisions in which diverse perspectives are forced to fit into politically framed solutions that may not meet the needs of the problem being solved. For example, when there is adamant advocacy by a very vocal member or one with social authority, some groups will agree too quickly in order to avoid confronting or displeasing a colleague. Sometimes a group member might remain silent or simply agree with a perspective or condone an action that he or she actually does not think is the best choice. In these cases, the best results of deep collaborative efforts are lost.

### Egocentric Constraints

When individual group members have high needs for control or low regard for the collective thought processes of the group, egocentric constraints influence interactions and outcomes. Individuals operating within such a framework foster a win/lose approach and spend their energy both advocating for their perspectives and proposals and criticizing others' perspectives and proposals. These behaviors are typical of Tuckman's (1965) storming stage of group development.

Balancing the tensions between autonomy and collaboration is difficult for some group members. A group member's individual needs trump group needs when he or she debates about process, monopolizes the conversation, and adamantly shares details to bolster arguments. Clear process agreements are necessary to minimize the negative effects of potential egocentric constraints on the group's dialogues, discussions, and decisions.

## The Tools for Talking

Skills with the tools for talking introduced in chapter 5 address the effects of Janis's (1989) constraints and are necessary resources for effective interaction. The skills are:

- Listen without judgment.
- Pause to create space for thinking.
- Paraphrase to support relationships, increase understanding, and mediate thinking.
- Inquire to focus and open thinking.

The frequency, pattern, and intention of tool use shift depending on the operating mode of discourse. In all cases, skillful application of this toolkit produces a safe and thoughtful environment for important conversations among colleagues.

*Listening for understanding is the foundation for all the other tools.*

Listening for understanding is the foundation for all the other tools. Without it, we don't know when to pause, what to paraphrase, or how to ask. Pauses are not just dead-air space; they are functional components of effective communication. Just as skillful listening requires internal discipline, pausing also demands active internal attention. In addition, waiting for a colleague to contribute, complete, or add a thought sends a message of high expectation and respect. The pause is also useful for maintaining emotional resourcefulness. During a pause, the metacognitive self-talk might include questions like, "Are my emotions clouding my thinking? Is my level of participation moving the group forward? What might be a useful next response here?"

While the tools are specialized, they work in concert. For example, a pattern of pausing, paraphrasing, and inquiring paces a conversation for thoughtfulness and high engagement. The pause allows for think time; the paraphrase clarifies the communication and links the responder's question to the speaker's statement. The inquiry opens or focuses thinking and often engages a specific cognitive process, such as comparison or prediction.

## Inviting Discourse

Skilled group members craft their communication to fully engage and support the cognitive and emotional resourcefulness of their colleagues. They use physical alignment, intonation, and syntax to invite discourse.

- **Physical alignment:** Postural alignment and gestural matching signal full attention. Nonverbal acknowledgements, such as nodding and smiling, and leaning in indicate acceptance for others' ideas.

- **Intonation:** Variations in inflection and pitch serve different purposes in skilled communications. A narrow range of modulation ending with a flat inflection at the end of the sentence suggests authority and certainty. In contrast, a pattern of wide modulation ending with a rising inflection is an approachable voice, suggesting tentativeness and curiosity. (See figure 6.2.) The former, or credible voice, is used for advocacy or to convey critical information the group needs to proceed. The approachable voice is used for inviting thinking, elaborating, and extending ideas (Grinder, 1997).

- **Syntax:** The way in which a speaker chooses and packages words is a powerful communication element, influencing the perception and interpretation of the message. Words are emotional and cognitive triggers, shaping the thoughts and responses of listeners.

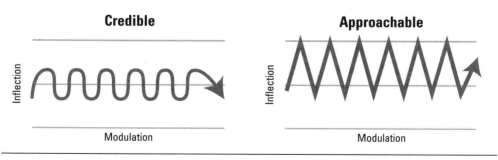

**Figure 6.2: Choosing voice.**

Asking someone to envision something creates an inventive, forward-thinking mindset. In contrast, asking someone to describe something suggests a more literal, present-minded response. As noted in chapter 5 (page 84), beginning questions with "Have you," "Did you," or "Can you" introduces doubt about readiness, capacity, or willingness. In contrast, starting inquiries with "How might you," "What are some," or "What might be some" communicates high expectations in readiness and capacity to explore. For example, see table 6.1.

**Table 6.1: Communicating High Expectations**

| Instead of Asking . . . | Try Asking . . . |
|---|---|
| "What is *the* most important trait to assess?" | "What are *some* important traits to assess?" |
| "How *could* we redesign this lesson?" | "How *might* we redesign this lesson?" |
| "What *is* causing these patterns?" | "What *seems* to be causing these patterns?" |
| "*Why* would we take time to do that?" | "*What* are some reasons to take time to do that?" |

### *Recognizing the Power of Presuppositions*

All communication carries both surface and embedded messages (Elgin, 2000). Each of these elements requires a listener to interpret. The subtle messages beneath the surface reveal a speaker's underlying assumptions, or presuppositions, about the listener's capacities. These messages are first processed emotionally; they influence both thought processes and the relationship between speakers and listeners. Positive presuppositions communicate a belief in listeners' readiness, willingness, and potential for bringing the best of themselves to the group and its work.

For example, compare the question, Does anyone see anything significant in these data?, with, Given your experience with literacy development, what are some things that stand out for you as you examine the data set? While the questions have the same intention (to bring attention to the data and what they might be indicating), the first form communicates doubt—in the group members' abilities and the data's significance. The latter form presupposes knowledge and experience, communicating belief in group members' willingness and readiness to carefully examine the data and respond to the inquiry. The power of positive presuppositions is that they inspire confidence and increase the thoughtfulness that group members bring to a topic. Table 6.2 illustrates the differences between dialogue, discussion, and decision making based on four comparators: purpose, process, outcome, and self-talk. (Self-talk describes the internalized questions skillful group members ask themselves in each mode.)

## Dialogue: Divergent Discourse for Opening Choice

Dialogue is an important first mode of discourse for group problem solving and decision making. When working with data, groups often rush to solutions before thoughtfully exploring the problem's dynamics. Expert groups apply the processes of dialogue to clarify and carefully frame problems before generating potential actions. In groups, these problem definitions emerge from multiple

**Table 6.2: Types of Discourse**

|  | **Dialogue** | **Discussion** | **Decision** |
|---|---|---|---|
| **Purpose** | Talking to understand and connect<br><br>Understanding the underlying nature of an issue and how group members perceive it | Talking to persuade and influence<br><br>Generating options<br><br>Clarifying outcomes | Talking to choose<br><br>Determining the best option from those the group generated |
| **Process (How)** | Speculating<br>Connecting<br>Theorizing<br>Visualizing | Reasoning<br>Comparing<br>Contrasting<br>Analyzing | Weighing<br>Choosing<br>Evaluating<br>Agreeing |
| **Outcome (What)** | Understanding | Weighing options<br>Choosing | Committing |
| **Self-Talk** | What is the deeper meaning?<br><br>What assumptions are operating here (for me and for others)?<br><br>What are some connections between these ideas?<br><br>What's not being said?<br><br>Are we all feeling safe enough to share? How can I increase the invitation to share? | What are the most important factors here?<br><br>How can I influence this interaction?<br><br>Are these data persuasive enough for me to let go of my ideas?<br><br>How are these ideas different from each other and from my own ideas?<br><br>What are the implications of this idea? | What is the weightiest item or criterion?<br><br>Which criteria are most important?<br><br>How do the options stack up against our criteria?<br><br>What are the pros and cons for each option?<br><br>What are the implications?<br><br>Who will be most affected? |

perspectives, differing frames of reference, and a variety of members' prior experiences. This exploration is best accomplished using dialogue.

In dialogue, group members listen and speak to understand one another's ideas, assumptions, beliefs, and values. A hallmark of dialogue is that group members are as invested in listening to others' ideas as they are in sharing their own ideas. The intention to understand does not imply agreement or disagreement: "dialogue seeks and explores the layers of meaning within ideas" (Wellman & Lipton, 2004, p. 39).

> *A hallmark of dialogue is that group members are as invested in listening to others' ideas as they are in sharing their own ideas.*

## Bringing Assumptions to the Surface

Assumptions matter; they govern perceptions, reveal beliefs and values, and ultimately form our criteria for right or wrong. As a result, assumptions are the roots of any dissonance when we feel oppositional to others' ideas. By externalizing and naming assumptions and hearing others', we emotionally distance ourselves from making judgments. Exploring assumptions provides a better understanding of what motivates us.

By naming our own assumptions, we make them available for inquiry and implicitly invite others to name theirs. This distancing from our assumptions frees us from the need to defend, creating emotional space to examine them. Trading defensiveness for curiosity allows for the psychological safety that produces shared understanding. Naming assumptions regarding student learning, teacher skill, curricular effectiveness, or home environment allows group members to examine them without needing to fight for agreement. Inquiring into assumptions would begin with a paraphrase and then might sound like, "What data or experience leads you to that assumption?" or "In what ways does this assumption influence our thinking about these data?"

# Discussion: Convergent Discourse for Clarifying Priorities

When groups transition to discussion, they begin to sort and select from a variety of possibilities that have the most merit. This process of analysis requires groups to compare and contrast different ideas. The discourse includes advocacy for particular ideas and persuasive arguments intended to influence the thinking of other group members. It also requires skillful inquiry into ideas for clarification, elaboration, and exploration of underlying assumptions.

What distinguishes skillful discussion from dysfunctional argument is agreement on clear outcomes that establish the purpose for talking. Adept groups avoid reasoning by anecdote and put data at the center as the primary source of information rather than personal opinions. Discussion is intended to lead to agreement: on the interpretation of the data, on possible solutions or actions, and on the meaning of key terms, such as *performance indicators*, *improve*, or *increase*. Skillful groups also invest energy in identifying unknown factors that might need to be pursued and questions that might need to be answered, such as, What elements have we not yet considered? or What might be some ripple effects of these interventions?

This mode of discourse requires attention to and careful application of the tools for talking. Paraphrasing becomes particularly important, establishing a pivot point for either inquiring into an idea or countering with an alternative idea. Inquiries still need to be invitational and not oppositional, thus tonal inflection and syntactical choices matter.

## Skillful Advocacy

To advocate is to speak for what you think or to speak for a point of view by making thinking transparent and available for others to examine. Advocacy uses logic and reason to persuade; it is a push for a preferred alternative.

Advocacy without inquiry into others' ideas and thoughts produces polarization, coalitions, defensive postures, and escalating vehemence. When group members exclusively advocate, the goal is to win the argument. When group members balance advocacy with inquiry, the goal is to collectively find the best argument. This reciprocal inquiry process establishes an atmosphere of shared vulnerability in which everyone's thinking is open to scrutiny, creating possibilities for learning by all (Senge, 1990). (See tables 6.3 and 6.4.)

**Table 6.3: Template for Advocacy—Making Thinking and Reasoning Visible**

| Describe the focus of your advocacy. | "An issue that is important to me is _____."<br>"I would like to focus our attention on _____."<br>"My assumptions are _____." |
|---|---|
| Describe your reasoning. | "I came to this conclusion because _____."<br>"As I thought about this, I recognized _____." |
| Describe your feelings. | "I feel _____ about this." |
| Distinguish data from interpretation. | "These are some observations that stand out for me in the data."<br>"Now here is what I think these data mean." |
| Reveal your perspective. | "I'm seeing this from the viewpoint of _____ or _____ or _____."<br>"Given my role and experience as a _____, . . ." |
| Frame the wider context that surrounds this issue. | "It occurs to me that this proposal would affect several groups: _____." |
| Give concrete examples. | "To get a clear picture, imagine that you are in School X and _____." |

*Source: Adapted from Senge, Kleiner, Roberts, & Ross, 1994.*

Visit **go.solution-tree.com/teams** for a reproducible version of this table.

**Table 6.4: Template for Advocacy—Inviting Others to Examine Your Thinking**

| Encourage others to explore your model, assumptions, and data. | "What is your thinking or reaction to what I just shared? What might be some flaws in my reasoning? What would you add or refine?" |
|---|---|
| Reveal where you are least clear. | "Here's an area that is fuzzy for me: _____. How would you describe it?" |
| Indicate your openness to the viewpoints of others. | "What are some different or alternate ways you see this?" |

*Source: Adapted from Senge et al., 1994.*

Visit **go.solution-tree.com/teams** for a reproducible version of this table.

# Decision Making: Convergent Discourse on Choice

To decide means to cut away options and finalize a choice. Decision-making groups work with the options selected during previous discussions. Skillful and thoughtful groups make skillful and thoughtful decisions. The seven qualities of high-performing groups we described in chapter 1, the collaborative learning cycle we described in chapter 2, and the stages of group development we described in chapter 5 provide foundational knowledge and approaches for working with data to make important decisions.

When a group convenes to make a decision, the preceding processes of dialogue and discussion create readiness for this often challenging phase of discourse. Carefully structuring and thoughtfully interacting within the collaborative learning cycle help group members manage the mental, emotional, and social challenges of making data-based decisions and crafting meaningful outcomes for their work. One essential element in effective decision making is clarity about both the process and the group members' roles and responsibilities in the selected process.

## Six Group Decision-Making Methods

Successful groups are clear about the decision-making processes that frame data-driven explorations and influence how people talk and listen to one another. Explicitness about the decision-making process is critical to this endeavor so the appropriate energy is focused on the task of working with data and on the relational needs of working with colleagues.

*No decision-making process is ideal. Depending on a group's history, skill level, and context, some group work will be more problematic, some more productive.*

There are six common decision-making methods (Schein, 1999). No decision-making process is ideal. Depending on a group's history, skill level, and context, some group work will be more problematic, some more productive. To increase effectiveness of application, the following list describes things to avoid and things to apply for each of these patterns.

1. **Decision by default:** When this occurs, the default is what Schein (1999) calls decision by *plop*. This often unlabeled decision-making method occurs when a group member suggests an idea, and before that proposal is examined another group member proposes a different idea, creating a random stack of ideas until the group selects one for action. The unsupported ideas lie in a heap of *plops* on the table or are left to die in the corners of the meeting room. In this circumstance, silence implicitly equals assent.

   To avoid this problem, group members need to be clear that they are at the point of decision making, illuminate a specific process for doing so, and be prepared to participate fully in the selected process.

2. **Decision by self-authorization:** Groups that do not formalize process fall victim to pressures from self-empowered individuals or coalitions within the group who push their agendas for action without regard for a sense of the larger group. Here again, the assumption is that silence means consent. *Groupthink* (Janis, 1982) is one well-studied form of decision by self-authorization. The group moves forward with an assumption of full agreement without checking to see whether silent group members are in accord with the proposal.

To avoid this problem, groups must create space for deliberation, inquire into a proposal, and preserve time for generating alternative courses of action.

3.  **Decision by external authority:** There are times when the group is not authorized to make the decision, and someone outside the group is the ultimate decider. In this case, the group's mandate is to both craft a recommendation and persuade those with decision-making authority. When lines of authority are fuzzy, groups invest energy, time, and emotion into honing a decision that outside agents may reject or modify.

    To avoid this problem, it is essential for the group to be clear about its role in the decision-making process: who is making the decision, and what information and presentation will have the most positive influence? In this way, the group can frame the recommendation in ways that will both inform and convince the decision maker.

4.  **Decision by majority vote:** This common decision-making method occurs in two forms: (1) when an informal poll is taken to get the sense of the group related to an issue, or (2) when someone makes a formal motion and puts the decision choices up for a vote. The liability for collaborative groups is that voting can create win/lose situations that then impede implementation or, in the worst cases, trigger noncompliance, or even sabotage.

    To avoid this problem, groups can elect a decision rule that mitigates these effects. One such rule is to establish super majority as the condition for reaching an agreement. Typically, this number is set at 75 percent of the full group. Another solution is for group members to apportion their vote across multiple options, for example, assigning percentages or dots to several choices within a list. This multivoting method reduces the win/lose dynamic and increases the likelihood that at least one of each group member's options will be chosen. (For a sample multivoting exercise to use with your group, see Spend-a-Buck, page 111.)

5.  **Decision by consensus:** Consensus requires sufficient time and structure for hearing all viewpoints. Consensus means that while all group members may not fully agree with a course of action, they are willing to move forward with a proposal and support it with integrity. A lack of time, tools, or willingness to speak up (such as when group members self-censor for fear that their comments and ideas might disrupt group harmony) limits the capacity for this method and can result in another form of *groupthink*. The silent pressure to conform distorts the process and hides potentially important information and insights from the group.

    To avoid this problem, group members need to develop and refine their discourse skills so that consensus decision making becomes a productive option. The rich patterns of dialogue and discussion embedded in the collaborative learning cycle establish a firm foundation for this decision process, establishing a sense of group members' ideas and perspectives. The opportunities for all group members to participate and find their voice ultimately develop shared understanding of issues and options, smoothing the transition to decision making by consensus.

6. **Decision by unanimous consent:** A common misconception is that complete agreement and commitment by all is the ideal. As groups develop, they discover that this method does not always make the best use of their time or energy. However, some decisions are so high stake that they do require unanimous consent from group members. Typically, these decisions involve major changes in practices or structures that affect critical working conditions. Most groups do not have the developmental readiness and skill levels needed to be effective with this mode of decision making.

To avoid this problem, groups can tap the skills of an external facilitator. A skilled facilitator can push a group's performance, structure for balanced participation, intervene when process breaks down, and move the group forward by framing expectations for the group and the task. Unanimous consent still requires high levels of discourse skill, fluency with shared structures and processes, and high levels of performance. Therefore for most decisions, consensus or some clear process for voting is the practical way to proceed.

Following are four tips to maximize productivity in the decision-making process.

1. Name and structure one mode of discourse at a time and mark clear transitions.

2. Name the boundaries—what is negotiable and non-negotiable in process and outcomes.

3. Name decision-making roles and responsibilities.

4. Name who will be most affected by a decision, and keep those people mentally and emotionally in the room.

### • • • • Data Story: Moving From Choice Points to Decision • • • •

At North Branch Middle School, the data team is using discipline referrals to explore the impact of its new behavior management program. Using the collaborative learning cycle to structure its meetings, it begins the activating and engaging phase with a dialogue that surfaces predictions and assumptions about what these data might show.

*Meeting One*

"I think the program is starting to make a difference, and we're going to see an overall decrease in office referrals."

"So, you're predicting fewer referrals. Which type of incidents do you think will have dropped the most?"

"I think it's either likely to be fewer fights or verbal disagreements. My assumption is that the hallway supervision is making teachers more visible during passing periods, and kids are responding to that."

"I agree that there will be a decrease. I think it's also because we are responding more immediately to language and tone—when it's positive and when it's negative."

"Then we have a similar prediction with two different assumptions; one about teacher presence, and the other about teacher feedback. What other predictions are we making?"

"I think kids are clearer about the consequences of acting out, but even so I predict that the chronic offenders won't have changed their behaviors."

"You're predicting the program has not affected the kids who typically are not complying with school rules. What are some assumptions about that?"

The group members continue their dialogue, charting their predictions and assumptions for another ten minutes without the data in front of them. They then move on to the exploring and discovering phase.

Circled around the data displays, the group continues its dialogue. Three graphs compare second-quarter and third-quarter referrals. One graph shows type of incident, time of day, and day of the week. Another is organized by incident and location. A third is a table listing referrals by student and infraction.

"One thing that really seems to pop out is a big drop overall on Fridays, which used to be a real crazy day."

"Look at this. Even though the number of fights hasn't changed, most of the other types of problems appear to be decreasing. Look at overt defiance. Last quarter there were twenty referrals, and this quarter we're down to fourteen."

"There were also fewer incidents overall in the hallways—a 20 percent drop, but no change in the common areas or the bus loading zone."

The group members continue to explore the data and chart their observations, including patterns, trends, and surprises.

Finally, toward the end of the session, they shift to a discussion about which observations would be most important to bring to the next phase of their work. They are intrigued by the contrast between behavior in the hallways and the other locations and determine to bring that back for further study. They also want to look more deeply at the incidents of fighting.

Moving on, they subdivide for the organizing and integrating phase. Each group takes one observation and generates causal theories.

*Group A: Locations of Infractions*

"I think most staff members are taking their responsibilities to be present in the hallways seriously, which explains why those numbers are dropping. My hunch is that fewer of us are as proactive about reinforcing expectations in the common areas and the bus loading zone."

"Your theory seems to be that this is a staff issue as much as it is a student issue. If that is the case, we need to gather data on how many teachers are at their hallway posts during passing periods and how they are interacting with kids."

"I think it's mostly a staff numbers issue in the common areas and the loading zone, so we need the same type of data for those places to help us sort that out."

"We need to set up a simple sampling system to record this information and bring that data to the next meeting."

*Group B: Incidents of Fighting*

"I think the incidents of fighting have stayed constant because those numbers represent the kids who have hair triggers and get into a lot of fights."

"So, you think there is a core group of kids who are not responding to the new program."

"We need to take a look at the specific students who are referred for fighting to confirm if this is the pattern before we plan further interventions."

They close the session by clarifying logistics for the next week's meeting.

### Meeting Two

After completing a focusing activity and re-establishing purpose, the group returns to the data.

"Let's look at the location data first. I think it's clear from the observation reports we collected that our theory about the differences between staff hallway patterns and the other two locations is pretty solid."

"Just to be clear here, you're seeing most staff members on duty in the hallways, and they are reinforcing our behavioral expectations as they interact with students."

"Yes, and based on the reports, there are not enough staff members in the common areas or supervising bus loading. At the loading zone, people are too busy getting kids lined up for the buses to have time to focus on positive behavioral interventions."

"Then we need to transfer the patterns of success in the hallways to those areas."

"Before we make a decision about that, let's look at the fighting data to see what they tell us."

It soon becomes apparent that this causal theory also holds up. That is, based on its continued data exploration, the team determines that the composition of the misbehaving students is the same, and the staff coverage is the variable that makes the difference in curtailing their behaviors. A stable group of students was involved in the majority of the fights during both of the recent quarters for which the members have data. The group agrees to move to decision making.

*The Decision Stage*

> "We first need to decide where to put our energy and consider who else needs to be involved and can help us work on the fighting issue because it's more complex than the other issues and will take longer to solve."

> "That makes sense. It would be important to get the counselors and administrators to join us for that discussion."

The group agrees to separate the issues and focus its efforts on the concerns about the common areas and bus loading zone.

> "I think we have two issues to solve here: one is the staffing issue, and the other is clarifying what those people will be doing while they are supervising those locations."

> "The staff are pretty stretched already. If we are going to propose a shift in duties, we need to develop some criteria for fairness. Not all duties are equal in the time and energy they require."

> "Your sense then is that we need to relook at the duties chart and add more specific descriptors or expectations of the supervisory duties at the high-infraction locations."

> "Yes, I think we need to build a chart and develop some weighted criteria for the demands of each duty. Then we can specify the adult behaviors that seem to have the greatest positive effects on student behavior."

> "So, we need to develop and include two key pieces of information in our recommendation to the staff: (1) clear descriptors of effective student supervisory practice in common areas and (2) a weighted criteria chart for fairly divvying up the supervisory duties."

The group continues, clarifying the details about who to involve in the redefinition of roles and identifying the additional information and resources it needs to clearly define the choice points and options involved in increasing staff coverage of critical areas. It also drafts a definition of *fairness* related to the relative weighting of staff duties to present to the faculty council for a decision on this key element of the plan to improve student behavior.

• • • • • • • • • • • • • • • • • • • • • • • • • • • • • • • • • • •

# Exercise Your Learning

Use your understanding of the dialogue, discussion, and decision modes of discourse to respond to the first two questions. Question three invites you to create a tool for assessing your group's use of the tools for talking and determining goal areas. Be sure to make the looks-like and sound-like lists observable behaviors.

1. **Think of a group topic:** When would dialogue be the most productive initial choice?

2. **Take a history lesson:** Think of decisions that went awry. What went wrong?

3. **Create a T-chart:** List the behaviors (looks like and sounds like) of a high-performing application of the tools for talking. Use your list as a self-assessment instrument. Compare your attributes to your group's present practices, identify gaps, and set growth goals.

## Extend Your Learning

The Co-Intelligence Institute (2003) shares definitions and guidelines for conducting effective dialogues (www.co-intelligence.org/P-dialogue.html).

The "Art of Powerful Questions" (Vogt, Brown, & Isaacs, 2003) is a free downloadable article from the developers of the World Café model for linking small-group interactions within a larger group to enhance creativity and idea development (www.theworldcafe.com/pdfs/aopq.pdf).

Co-Creative Power (www.myriam-musing.blogspot.com) is Myriam Laberge's blog on facilitation. She reflects on effective meetings, public engagement, dialogue, and conversations.

The Center for Graphic Facilitation (http://graphicfacilitation.blogs.com) provides links to sample graphics, videos, articles, tips, learning events, and resource people.

Visit **go.solution-tree.com/teams** to access the links to the materials mentioned in this book.

# Spend-a-Buck

## Purpose

Spend-a-Buck is a useful self-assessment tool used at a midpoint in a project or learning series. It helps individuals and groups determine relative priorities within a list of options, interests, or actions. Each group member is offered an *imaginary* stack of one hundred pennies to "spend" across the items of choice.

## Benefit

This strategy promotes choice making and personalization. It allows individuals to reflect on their own preferences, strengths, and interests. Spend-a-Buck also supports group members in appreciating the variety of interests and perspectives of others.

## Logistics

### Materials and Preparation
- Recording sheet with options listed (if known ahead of time)
- Chart paper for master list

### Time
- Ten to fifteen minutes depending on group size

### Grouping
- Full group

## Instructions

1. Display a slide or chart that presents the options, actions, or interest areas of choice. Distribute recording sheets listing the options.

2. Describe the Spend-a-Buck procedure: Participants may "spend" as many or as few of their pennies for each option as they desire. The goal is to create as clear a representation as possible of their personal interests.

3. With a calculator in hand, have each group member tally and report the number of pennies he or she spent for each item. Add these together, and record the group's total for each item on a public chart. This is especially useful if the group is using Spend-a-Buck as a decision-making tool.

4. Form task groups or learning groups by having people join others with similar interests per the public chart. Note: Group members without strong preferences or needs can then balance out the numbers in the subgroups.

page 1 of 2

## Example of a Tally

Professional development study-group options—

| | |
|---|---:|
| *Differentiated learning* | *33* |
| *Technology integration* | *24* |
| *Reading in the content areas* | *21* |
| *Formative assessment* | *22* |
| | *100* |

**Variation:** Give each participant one hundred sticky dots to place on a public chart. This is especially important when group members need to see the relative support for options and proposed actions.

*Source: Lipton & Wellman, 2011a.*

# CHAPTER SEVEN

# *Evolving Decisions Into Actions*

Decisions are not plans, and plans are not actions. Skillful discourse and data work within the collaborative learning cycle lead groups to agree on a general course of action. While this process adjusts the compass to the desired direction, it does not create the map or plot the journey. Thoughtful designs are bridges between solutions that emerge from the collaborative learning cycle and outcome-driven actions that bring fresh approaches to student learning issues.

## Common Barriers to Effective Planning

Efficient planning requires discipline and attention to process. The hectic pace of typical school days and limited time for teamwork push against the need for deliberation and sufficient emotional distance that successful designs for action draw on. When groups lack perspective, they fall into three common planning traps.

> *Thoughtful designs are bridges between solutions that emerge from the collaborative learning cycle and outcome-driven actions that bring fresh approaches to student learning issues.*

1. **Acting impulsively:** Being busy is not the same as being effective. Groups often react to self-imposed or externally driven pressure to do something. This well-intended response deters a group's effectiveness in the planning process. In the rush to action, important details are overlooked. Taking a step back and summoning the critical affective and cognitive resources to plan thoughtfully are important here. Slowing down at this point saves time in effective implementation.

2. **Confusing activity with outcome:** Activity-driven planning focuses energy on action, not results. When the activity becomes an end in itself, there is rigidity in approach and vagueness in outcome. Many well-intended intervention efforts suffer from this habit because of the emotional need to take action. Doing anything feels better than doing nothing.

3. **Lurching from problem to program:** Adopting a program is not a plan. It is rare that a prepackaged approach addresses the specific dimensions of a local problem. This quick-fix mentality and search for off-

the-shelf solutions misdirect planning energy. Minimally, programs need to be thoughtfully tailored to fit a particular context. More often, planning groups need to develop local strategies or adapt available resources to address complex conditions.

## Elements of an Effective Plan

Comprehensive planning addresses the three common effective-planning barriers. These effective plans have several critical features. These elements determine the timeline for each task, describing what needs to be done in what order, how long each step should take, and who will be primarily responsible. The elements of an effective plan are the following.

- **Clear outcomes:** Clarity of outcomes is the most important part of any planning process. This requires specificity and understanding of success criteria.

- **Sequence and timelines:** Workable plans detail the sequence of actions that need to occur across the project's timeline. This essential planning element calibrates actions with time frames to ensure reasonable pacing.

- **Monitoring systems:** Monitoring systems provide a mechanism for assessing progress and guiding any necessary course corrections. Effective plans identify key benchmarks across the implementation timeline and multiple measures for accomplishing this function.

- **Roles and responsibilities:** Plans for programs that endure clearly delineate tasks and duties—who will do what, how, and by when. This specificity applies to all aspects of implementing and monitoring the innovation or intervention.

The first element—clear outcomes—drives the rest of the process in effective planning. Given the complexity of persistent problems, planning groups often need to focus their goals and create multiple outcomes that build toward desired results. These outcomes describe measures of progress within one- to three-year time frames at district, school, and classroom levels.

## Smart Plans Require SMART Goals

One field-tested approach for clarifying outcomes is to create SMART goals (O'Neill & Conzemius, 2006). The letters stand for specific and strategic, measurable, attainable, results oriented, and time bound. Together these five qualities provide an organizing template for groups to collaboratively generate clear goals.

The following questions support the development of SMART goals.

- **Specific and strategic:** To determine if your goal is specific and strategic, ask the following: "What is the greatest area of need? What knowledge, skills, and dispositions do we need to address? What are the criteria for success?"

- **Measureable:** To determine if your goal is measurable, ask the following: "As we are progressing, what will we see or hear? Where and when? In student products and performances? When our goal is achieved, what will we see or hear? Where and when? In student products and performances? What tools will we use to measure progress?"

- **Attainable:** To determine if your goal is attainable, ask the following: "Given the gap between present performance and desired results, what is achievable? Given our resources, what are reasonable increments for improvement?"

- **Results oriented:** To determine if your goal is results oriented, ask the following: "Are we keeping the end in mind or getting lost in describing the process? In what ways do these goals align with other goals for the district, school, team, and so on?"

- **Time bound:** To determine if your goal is time bound, ask the following: "What is our time frame for achievement? At what points will we gather data to determine progress?"

SMART goals focus on the few things most likely to have the greatest impact, have both short- and long-term impact, align with other key strategic initiatives, and target results. See table 7.1 for examples of fuzzy goals and SMART goals.

**Table 7.1: From Fuzzy to SMART Goals**

| Fuzzy Goals | SMART Goals |
|---|---|
| Fifth-grade students will improve their reading skills. | Within two years, 80 percent of grade 5 students will be at or above proficiency level in comprehension skills. |
| We will have a decrease in dropout rates by next June. | Within three years, the high school graduation rate will increase to 90 percent of our students. |
| We will improve oral language skills for English learners. | Over the next three years, we will increase the number of students who can demonstrate mastery of oral language proficiency from 24 percent to 75 percent. |

# Intervention Planning Template: A Graphic Planning Tool

An intervention planning template (IPT) is a graphic tool for focusing the group's thinking on one element of the planning process at a time. SMART goals are embedded within this framework. It operates on the principles of backward design. By starting with the end in mind, planning teams work backward step-by-step to construct the plan. The intention is to keep the focus on the desired student behaviors (focus of improvement) and visualize the support systems (growth agents) student and teachers require to produce those behaviors. Outcome maps such as this are effective because they isolate each step, producing both clarity and agreement before moving on. Using IPTs, the group identifies the specific behaviors that provide a scaffold for targeting action. Although the process maps backward from the desired results, it moves the thinking forward, shifting attention from existing conditions to identified outcomes. Using public charting and visual support provides a third point for group engagement.

For example, as a result of applying the collaborative learning cycle, a group has made a decision. It has defined and agreed on an action arena—addressing disrespectful behavior or improving students' problem-solving skills. That is, it makes a decision about which course of action to pursue. The IPT outlines the specific details that need to be incorporated into the plan. To construct an IPT, work from right to left (step one to step eight). (See figures 7.1 and 7.2 for examples.)

| Growth Agents | | | | Focus of Improvement | | | |
|---|---|---|---|---|---|---|---|
| Step 8 | Step 7 | Step 6 | Step 5 | Step 4 | Step 3 | Step 2 | Step 1 *Start here. |
| Required team knowledge, skills, and dispositions | Desired team products and performances (SMART goal) | Required teacher knowledge, skills, and dispositions | Desired teaching products and performances (SMART goal) | Required student knowledge, skills, and dispositions | Desired student products and performances (SMART goal) | Broad outcome | Identified action arena |
|  |  |  |  |  |  |  |  |

**Figure 7.1: Sample intervention planning template.**

1. Transfer an identified action arena (from previous work sessions).
2. State the desired outcome in a positive term (what you want to have happen, not what you want to eliminate or reduce).
3. Identify and clarify success criteria and indicators for the desired student products and performances (what would you want to see or hear—SMART goals).
4. Identify the essential knowledge, skills, and dispositions students need to achieve the success criteria. (Each SMART goal in step three requires its own set of knowledge, skills, and dispositions. It is usually best to select the two or three most catalytic goals and focus energy on these.)

| Growth Agents | | | | Focus of Improvement | | | |
|---|---|---|---|---|---|---|---|
| Step 8 | Step 7 | Step 6 | Step 5 | Step 4 | Step 3 | Step 2 | Step 1 **\*Start here.** |
| Required team knowledge, skills, and dispositions | Desired team products and performances (SMART goal) | Required teacher knowledge, skills, and dispositions | Desired teaching products and performances (SMART goal) | Required student knowledge, skills, and dispositions | Desired student products and performances (SMART goal) | Broad outcome | Identified action arena |
| Collaborative skills for co-developing and modifying lessons and assessments<br><br>Willingness to reveal knowledge gaps about teaching reading comprehension and math computational fluency<br><br>Persistence and continued focus on implementing the plan of action | The grade 5 team will develop sample word problems for instructional use by all team members on a weekly basis and modify these as needed to reinforce and develop student skills, based on formative assessments.<br><br>Teachers will share instructional strategies and adaptations for reading comprehension and math computation skill development on a weekly basis.<br><br>Teachers will develop and share formative assessments that isolate needed specific subskills in reading and math that emerge from student work produced by the weekly assignments. | Knowledge of instructional strategies for developing reading comprehension and reasoning skills including: vocabulary, main idea identification, and interpretation of text<br><br>Willingness to learn from and modify decisions and choices that the group is making<br><br>Fluency with strategies for introducing and reinforcing math concepts and operational skills<br><br>Formative assessment skills for regularly checking for student understanding to identify students who may still be struggling<br><br>Patience and persistence with staying the course | Direct teaching and modeling of comprehension and reasoning skills with sample problems selected and developed by the grade 5 team<br><br>Computational practice on a daily basis by all students to develop fluency and accuracy<br><br>Direct teaching and modeling of estimating and checking for accuracy with sample problems developed by the grade 5 team, including problems with wrong answers | Reading comprehension skills for identifying key words and phrases and interpreting their meaning in word problems<br><br>Reasoning skills for determining the appropriate computational operations<br><br>Computational fluency and accuracy<br><br>Reasonableness of answers | 85 percent of students will accurately solve math word problems on the spring benchmark assessment | Students will improve their abilities to interpret and solve math word problems | Grade 5 math word problems |

**Figure 7.2: Sample completed intervention planning template.**

5. Identify and clarify success criteria and indicators for the desired teacher products and performances (what would you want to see or hear) to support and produce student success.

6. Identify the essential knowledge, skills, and dispositions teachers need to achieve the success criteria.

7. Identify and clarify success criteria and indicators for the desired team products and performances to support and produce the teacher success (what would you want to see or hear).

8. Identify the essential knowledge, skills, and dispositions teams need to achieve the success criteria.

Once the data team has clarified goals and success indicators, the remaining plan elements can be determined: access or develop measurement tools, establish sequence and time frames, and assign roles and responsibilities. The plan is then ready for implementation.

We offer ten tips for successful planning.

1. **Be specific:** Vague aspirations lead to unfocused implementation. A plan can't be too explicit. The more detailed the descriptors and indicators, the clearer the picture of success will be for all roles—team members, teachers, and students.

2. **Split rather than lump outcomes:** Groups often try to plan for too big an action arena without breaking down the issue into multiple outcomes. For example, to address a reading comprehension goal, the plan would track backward from separate and simultaneous outcomes, one for improving literal comprehension skills and one for improving inferential comprehension skills.

3. **Assign a champion:** When *everyone* is responsible, communication is inefficient, task assignment is unclear, and energy is wasted. While everyone may be passionate about goal achievement, someone needs to be responsible for plan management. This point person has primary responsibility for specific tasks, such as collecting and organizing data for review, informing the larger group, gathering resources, and monitoring deadlines.

4. **Anticipate barriers:** Technological and logistical glitches are inevitable. Some groups lose heart when they encounter technical, political, and sociological obstacles as they implement their plan. The need for planning means that there is a need for change. All organizations naturally resist change. By anticipating potential barriers, groups can more thoughtfully plan for both successful implementation and effective communication with all parties affected by the plan.

5. **Sell the problem, not the solution:** When all involved both understand and own the problem that motivated the plan, they are less likely to

fight the changes involved with the proposed solution. Strategically use compelling data and anecdotal evidence for this purpose.

6.   **Beware the quick fix:** When timelines for success are too short or goals are too big, groups are drawn to quick-fix solutions. Typically, these treat the symptoms of a problem but are usually not robust enough to address causal factors that may be producing those symptoms. Lasting change takes time to implement thoroughly.

> *When timelines for success are too short or goals are too big, groups are drawn to quick-fix solutions.*

7.   **Monitor frequently and consistently:** Plans are hazy desires if they are not monitored regularly. Groups should identify and build in benchmarks and short-cycle assessments into plans. These data become gauges by which the planning group then adjusts its efforts and interventions.

8.   **Expect an implementation dip:** Improvement is not always a steady upward climb. There will be dips and valleys as teachers and students let go of former behaviors and practice new approaches to teaching and learning. The inevitable dips are opportunities for clarifying and refocusing efforts with the established outcomes in mind.

9.   **See plateaus as opportunities to consolidate gains:** Just as dips occur, growth also plateaus as the first-level effects of the plan take hold. These plateaus are times to consolidate current effective practices and ensure that all involved are using them. This consolidation establishes a firm foundation for the next growth spurt.

10.   **Design for sustainability:** Plans that are initially successful often flounder when personnel change or fresh problems emerge that divert energy from implementation efforts. Effective planning groups design for sustainability when they induct new members by training and mentoring them in the established practices, ensure a program champion, and maintain a consistent monitoring system.

# Planning as a Learning Process, and Learning as a Planning Process

Groups that learn from their planning pay attention to both the task and the process as they learn with and from one another. Planning for instructional improvement requires teachers to delve deeply into both content and pedagogical knowledge. As teachers do so, they inevitably confront their beliefs about teaching, learning, and learners, understanding more about themselves and their colleagues. Collaborative planning also demands pushing past personal preferences, stretching outside of comfort zones, and inviting others to do so as well.

A collaborative planning process produces unexpected perspectives and potential causal theories. These surprises emerge from data-driven inquiry.

High-performing groups learn to welcome these surprises, because they foster fresh looks at old ways and require teachers to revisit curriculum pathways and teaching approaches that may be producing performance gaps. A collaborative planning process also opens up the range of potential choices for action. Working together, groups exercise the discipline of productive planning: to rethink core curriculum and instructional patterns before developing interventions to address immediate student concerns.

Thoughtful data work reveals gaps in student performance that ultimately lead to recognition of gaps in instructional repertoire. Healthy groups are careful not to turn cause-and-effect analysis into a blame game. Rather, they summon the resources to clarify gaps, research appropriate instructional approaches, and craft implementation plans to address central issues. Ultimately student learning emerges from teacher learning. This rich learning results from productive collaborative planning processes.

• • • • • • • **Data Story: Planning With SMART Goals** • • • • • • •

Based on its exploration and analysis of several data sources, the science department at Fairview High School has decided to work on improving student inquiry skills across the science curriculum. The team's teachers intend to revise the way they teach experimental design by including explicit instruction on the fundamental thinking skills required. The focus of their weekly work session is to create SMART goals to launch the planning process. They put chart paper on the wall to publicly record the ideas as they develop, and they begin by restating the action arena: science inquiry skills and abilities to design investigations of natural phenomena. The discussion begins.

> "That's really broad. I think we should separate that into at least two goals—one about design and then maybe some about specific inquiry skills."

> "Fine. Let's first clarify what we mean by *design*. To me, it's being able to craft testable questions or construct hypotheses."

> "Yes, and also a big part is that kids are able to identify variables and build in controls by testing one factor while holding others constant."

> "Prediction is important here too. We're talking about inference skills, and they both relate to the ability to hypothesize."

One group member moves to the chart where a template for SMART goals has been set up to keep the five elements in focus, and he starts a rough draft:

> *Students will be able to create experimental designs by predicting, inferring, and hypothesizing.*

> "It needs to be more specific. How about adding something about testable questions?"

> *Students will be able to craft testable questions to create experimental designs by predicting, inferring, and hypothesizing.*

"The thinking skills shouldn't be part of the goal statement. Let's make the goal be about the product—testable questions and experimental designs. So, it might read: *Students will be able to create experimental designs that include testable questions with identified control variables.*"

"That's good. We also need some measurement and time frames."

"Try this: *By the end of next semester, 90 percent of our students in grades 9–12 will be able to create experimental designs that include testable questions with identified control variables.*"

"OK. We've got a clear goal statement. Now, what would we look for, and how will we collect data to determine how we're doing?"

With the agreed-on goal statement on the first chart, the group continues by mapping backward, naming the success criteria that define proficiency in experimental design and the specific indicators it would look for as students are working toward goal achievement.

"So, we agree that each of us will be responsible for designing and collecting student products as formative assessments and will bring back some samples to search for patterns."

The group creates a subcommittee to develop a measurement tool that can be used across all specialty areas to assess students' work and creates a calendar for upcoming meetings where it'll explore the classroom-based data.

"So, next steps are for us to get together to plan, or maybe revise, units in our own areas that include instruction on experimental design that targets the specific thinking skills we're looking for. Then we need to select some student work that we'll bring back to analyze at our next meeting."

• • • • • • • • • • • • • • • • • • • • • • • • • • • • • • • • • • • • •

# Exercise Your Learning

Use the following exercises and reproducibles to apply the structures and tools described in this chapter in your own work.

1. Based on a current issue in your work site, craft two or three SMART goals to begin action planning. Visit **go.solution-tree.com/plcbooks** and use the SMART goals reproducibles in *Learning by Doing* (DuFour et al., 2010) to guide your work.

2. Use the Intervention Planning Template (page 123) to create a template for a specific action arena.

# Extend Your Learning

A group decision-making toolkit is available from the Iowa State University Extension (2001) service (www.extension.iastate.edu/communities/tools /decisions). The site has links with clear explanations of the following tools: brainstorming, nominal group technique, paired comparisons, card sort technique, Charette procedure, and storyboarding.

Gantt and PERT Charts (http://gates.comm.virginia.edu/rrn2n/teaching /gantt.htm) are tools for visualizing the steps required for successful project planning. Charles Gantt developed his method in 1917 as a way of envisioning the sequence of tasks across a timeline. The U.S. Navy developed PERT (Program Evaluation and Review Technique) in the 1950s for planning complex projects with high degrees of interdependency between tasks (Nelson, 2009).

As discussed in chapter 3, Mind Tools offers a wide variety of management, career, and thinking tools. Visit www.mindtools.com/pages/main/newMN _TED.htm for a practical set of decision-making tools and short articles (Mind Tools, n.d.b).

Multivoting is a technique for winnowing lists of options. It efficiently helps a group to narrow choices and preserve the sense of harmony that is often disrupted by majority voting. In one common form of multivoting, each participant is assigned a number of votes equaling one-third of the number of items on the list. This vote may be repeated as the list shortens. See www.doh.state .fl.us/hpi/pdf/MultiVoting2.pdf (Florida Department of Health, Office of Performance Improvement, n.d.) for more information. This article elaborates on several practical forms of multivoting and offers ideas for their application.

As mentioned in chapter 6 (page 105), another version of multivoting involves using sticky dots or sticky notes. Participants are assigned a number of sticky dots and may apportion their dots as they see fit by assigning more than one dot to a choice. One useful rule is that participants may not assign all of their dots to one item.

# Intervention Planning Template

| Focus of Improvement | | | | | Growth Agents | | | |
|---|---|---|---|---|---|---|---|---|
| Step 1 *Start here. | Step 2 | Step 3 | Step 4 | Step 5 | Step 6 | Step 7 | Step 8 | |
| Identified action arena | Broad outcome | Desired student products and performances (SMART goal) | Required student knowledge, skills, and dispositions | Desired teaching products and performances (SMART goal) | Required teacher knowledge, skills, and dispositions | Desired team products and performances (SMART goal) | Required team knowledge, skills, and dispositions | |
| | | | | | | | | |

# References and Resources

American Society for Quality. (n.d.). *Cause analysis tools: Pareto chart.* Accessed at http://asq.org/learn-about-quality/cause-analysis-tools /overview/pareto.html on October 13, 2011.

Beach, L. (1997). *The psychology of decision making: People in organizations.* Thousand Oaks, CA: SAGE.

Bolam, R., McMahon, A., Stoll, L., Thomas, S., & Wallace, M. (2005). *Creating and sustaining effective professional learning communities* (Research Brief No. RR637). London: Department for Education and Skills. Accessed at www.education.gov.uk/publications/eOrdering Download/RR637-2.pdf on September 8, 2011.

Co-Intelligence Institute. (2003). *Dialogue.* Accessed at www.co-intelligence .org/P-dialogue.html on October 13, 2011.

Creative Research Systems. (2011). *The survey systems tutorial: Survey design.* Accessed at www.surveysystem.com/sdesign.htm on May 17, 2011.

Deal, T., & Peterson, K. (1999). *Shaping school culture: The heart of leadership.* San Francisco: Jossey-Bass.

DuFour, R., DuFour, R., Eaker, R., & Many, T. (2010). *Learning by doing: A handbook for professional learning communities at work* (2nd ed.). Bloomington, IN: Solution Tree Press.

Elgin, S. (2000). *The gentle art of verbal self-defense.* New York: Prentice Hall.

Few, S. (2004). *Show me the numbers: Designing tables and graphs to enlighten.* Oakland, CA: Analytics Press.

Few, S. (2009). *Now you see it: Simple visualization techniques for quantitative analysis.* Oakland, CA: Analytics Press.

Florida Department of Health, Office of Performance Improvement. (n.d.). *Multivoting.* Accessed at www.doh.state.fl.us/hpi/pdf/MultiVoting2 .pdf on October 25, 2011.

Goddard, R., Hoy, W. K., & Woolfolk Hoy, A. W. (2000). Collective teacher efficacy: Its meaning, measure, and impact on student achievement. *American Educational Research Journal, 37*(2), 479–507.

Goddard, R., Hoy, W. K., & Woolfolk Hoy, A. W. (2004). Collective efficacy beliefs: Theoretical developments, empirical evidence, and future directions. *Educational Researcher, 33*(3), 3–13.

Goldberg, M. C. (1998). *The art of the question: A guide to short-term question-centered therapy.* New York: Wiley.

Greenspan, A. (2007). *The age of turbulence.* New York: Penguin.

Grinder, M. (1997). *The science of non-verbal communication album: The elusive obvious.* Battle Ground, WA: Grinder.

Hajek, J. (2009, July 17). *Cause and effect diagram training video* [Video file]. Accessed at www.youtube.com/watch?v=bNDlg1h-za0 on October 13, 2011.

Hargreaves, A., & Shirley, D. (2009). The persistence of presentism. *Teachers College Record, 111*(11), 2505–2534.

Herman, J., & Winters, L. S. (1992). *Tracking your school's success: A guide to sensible evaluation.* Thousand Oaks, CA: Corwin Press.

Hoy, W., Tarter, J., & Woolfolk Hoy, A. (2006). Academic optimism in schools: A force for student achievement. *American Educational Research Journal, 43*(3), 425–446.

Ingram, D., Louis, K. R. S., & Schroeder, R. (2004). Accountability policies and teacher decision making: Barriers to the use of data to improve practice. *Teachers College Record, 106*(6), 1258–1287.

Integrated Performance Leadership Group. (2007). *5 whys root cause analysis worksheet: A back to the basics improvement template.* Bokeelia, FL: Author. Accessed at www.theiplgroup.com/5%20Whys%20Template .pdf on January 16, 2012.

Iowa State University Extension. (2001). *Group decision making tool kit.* Accessed at www.extension.iastate.edu/communities/tools/decisions on October 25, 2011.

Janis, I. (1982). *Groupthink: Psychological studies of policy decisions and fiascoes* (2nd ed.). Boston: Houghton Mifflin.

Janis, I. (1989). *Crucial decisions: Leadership in policymaking and crisis management.* New York: Free Press.

Jaques, J., & Cason, K. (1994). *Human capability: A study of individual potential and its application.* Falls Church, VA: Cason Hall.

Johnson, R. S., & Avelar La Salle, R. (2010). *Data strategies to uncover and eliminate hidden inequities: The wallpaper effect.* Thousand Oaks, CA: Corwin Press.

Kastner, M. (2009a). *10 common flaws in math tests.* Accessed at http://marciakastner.com/10-common-flaws-in-math-tests_289.html on October 25, 2011.

Kastner, M. (2009b). *Testing the test: Actual bad questions.* Accessed at www.marciakastner.com/actual-bad-questions_300.html on May 16, 2011.

Lipton, L., & Wellman, B. (2010). *Data-driven dialogue: Practical strategies for collaborative inquiry.* Sherman, CT: MiraVia. Accessed at http://miravia.com/documents/DDDInstituteSpring2010.pdf on November 29, 2011.

Lipton, L., & Wellman, B. (2011a). *Groups at work: Strategies and structures for professional learning.* Sherman, CT: MiraVia.

Lipton, L., & Wellman, B. (2011b). *Leading groups: Effective strategies for building professional community.* Sherman, CT: MiraVia.

Louis, K. S., & Marks, H. (1998). Does professional community affect the classroom? Teachers' work and student work experiences in restructuring schools. *American Journal of Education, 106*(4), 532–575.

McDonough, M. (2011). *Creating Pareto charts with Microsoft Excel.* Accessed at www.brighthub.com/office/project-management/articles/8708.aspx on October 13, 2011.

McLaughlin, M. W. (2011). Shifts in reform influence how and what teachers learn. *Phi Delta Kappan, 92*(6), 67.

McLaughlin, M. W., & Talbert, J. E. (1993). *Contexts that matter for teaching and learning: Strategic opportunities for meeting the nation's education goals.* Stanford, CA: Stanford University Center for Research on the Context of Secondary School Teaching.

McLaughlin, M. W., & Talbert, J. E. (2001). *Professional communities and the work of high school teaching.* Chicago: University of Chicago Press.

Minahan, M., & Hutton, C. (2002). Group development tools practitioners can use. *OD Practitioner, 34*(3), 31–35. Accessed at www.ntl.org/upload/GroupDevelopmentTools.pdf on January 16, 2012

Mind Tools. (n.d.a). *Belbin's team roles: Understanding team roles to improve performance.* Accessed at www.mindtools.com/pages/article/newLDR_83.htm on January 5, 2012.

Mind Tools. (n.d.b). *Decision making techniques: How to make better decisions.* Accessed at www.mindtools.com/pages/main/newMN_TED.htm on October 13, 2011.

Mind Tools. (n.d.c). *5 whys: Quickly getting to the root of a problem.* Accessed at www.mindtools.com/pages/article/newTMC_5W.htm on October 13, 2011.

Nelson, R. R. (2009). *Gantt and PERT charts.* Accessed at http://gates.comm.virginia.edu/rrn2n/teaching/gantt.htm on October 13, 2011.

Newman, F. M., King, M. B., & Rigdon, M. (1997). Accountability and school performance: Implications for restructuring schools. *Harvard Educational Review, 67*(1), 41–74.

O'Neill, J., & Conzemius, A. (2006). *The power of SMART goals: Using goals to improve student learning.* Bloomington, IN: Solution Tree Press.

Pacanowsky, M. (1995). Team tools for wicked problems. *Organizational Dynamics, 23*(3), 36–51.

Peterson, K., & Deal, T. (2009). *The shaping school culture fieldbook.* San Francisco: Jossey-Bass.

Rowe, M. B. (1986). Wait time: Slowing down may be a way of speeding up! *Journal of Teacher Education, 37*(1), 43–49.

Schein, E. H. (1999). *Process consultation revisited: Building the helping relationship.* Reading, MA: Addison-Wesley.

Schein, E. H. (2004). *Organizational culture and leadership* (3rd ed.). San Francisco: Jossey-Bass.

Schwarz, R. (2002). *The skilled facilitator: A comprehensive resource for consultants, facilitators, managers, trainers, and coaches.* San Francisco: Jossey-Bass.

Senge, P. (1990). *The fifth discipline: The art and practice of the learning organization.* New York: Doubleday.

Senge, P., Kleiner, A., Roberts, C., & Ross, R. (1994). *The fifth discipline fieldbook: Strategies and tools for building a learning organization.* New York: Crown Business.

Smith, M. K. (2005). Bruce W. Tuckman—forming, storming, norming and performing in groups. *The Encyclopædia of Informal Education.* Accessed at www.infed.org/thinkers/tuckman.htm on March 7, 2011.

Thurber, J. (1939, March 18). The secret life of Walter Mitty. *The New Yorker,* p. 19.

Tschannen-Moran, M. (2004). *Trust matters: Leadership for successful schools.* San Francisco: Jossey-Bass.

Tuckman, B. W. (1965). Developmental sequence in small groups. *Psychological Bulletin, 63,* 384–399.

Tuckman, B. W., & Jensen, M. A. C. (1977). Stages of small-group development revisited. *Group and Organization Management, 2*(4), 419–427.

Tufte, E. R. (1983). *The visual display of quantitative information.* Cheshire, CT: Graphics Press.

Vogt, E. E., Brown, J., & Isaacs, D. (2003). *The art of powerful questions: Catalyzing insight, innovation, and action.* Mill Valley, CA: Whole Systems. Accessed at www.theworldcafe.com/pdfs/aopq.pdf on October 13, 2011.

Weick, K. E. (1995). *Sensemaking in organizations.* Thousand Oaks, CA: SAGE.

Wellman, B., & Lipton, L. (2004). *Data-driven dialogue: A facilitator's guide to collaborative inquiry.* Sherman, CT: MiraVia.

Wiliam, D. (2011). *Embedded formative assessment.* Bloomington, IN: Solution Tree Press.

Windle, R., & Warren, S. (n.d.). *Communication skills.* Accessed at www.directionservice.org/cadre/section4.cfm on March 7, 2011.

# *Index*

## A

action, 34
activating and engaging, 25
    potential, 27–28
    process, 27
    purpose of, 26
    result of skipping, 28
    tips for success, 28–29
advocacy, skillful, 102–103
affiliative constraints, 97–98
American Society for Quality (ASQ),
    49–50
archival data, 35, 64–65
"Art of Powerful Questions, The"
    (Vogt, Brown, and Isaacs), 110
assessment
    formative, 56
    group, 85, 88–90
    summative, 56
assumptions, communication,
    101–102
assumptions and predictions
    concurrent development of, 29
    distinguishing between, 28–29
    record keeping, 29
authority, decision making by
    external, 105
autonomy-collaboration, work-style
    preference, 77
autonomy to collaboration, shift
    from, 7–8

## B

bar graphs, 67
behavioral data collection, 62
Belbin, M., 20
Bion, W., 87
birdwalk alert, 12
body language, 99
bounded rationality, 97

## C

box plots, 67
Bright Hub, 50
Brown, J., 110

causation
    correlation versus, 44–45
    theories/categories of, 33–34,
        46–48
cause-and-effect diagrams, 49
Center for Graphic Facilitation, 110
certainty-ambiguity, 77
close-up questions, 61
Co-Creative Power, 110
cognitive constraints, 97
Co-Intelligence Institute, 110
collaboration, shift from autonomy
    to, 7–8
collaborative cultures, promises and
    problems of, 2–3
collaborative learning cycle
    activating and engaging, 25, 26–29
    example of, 36–37
    exploring and discovering, 25, 26,
        29–32
    organizing and integrating, 25, 26,
        33–36
    summary of, 26
commitment, 10, 13
committee without community, 2
communication
    assumptions, 101–102
    body language, 99
    constraints for productive, 96–98
    decision making, 95, 100, 101,
        103–106
    dialogue, 95, 100–102
    discussion, 95, 100, 101, 102–103
    example of, 106–109
    intonation/voice, 99
    presuppositions, 100

language used in, 32
role of effective, 65–66
types of graphic formats, 67
DuFour, R., 3

# E

egocentric constraints, 98
80/20 rule, 50
equity, group, 14
exploring and discovering, 25, 26
pitfalls, 31
potential, 30–31
process, 30
purpose of, 29–30
tips for success, 31–32

# F

feasibility, 64
feedback, 15–17
Few, S., 68, 70
fishbone diagrams, 49
"5 Whys Root Cause Analysis," 49
focus, 10, 11–12
formative assessment/data, 56
forming, 78, 79

# G

gaming the system, 9
Gantt charts, 122
goals, SMART, 36, 114–115, 120–121
Goldberg, M. C., 12
Gore, B., 29–30
"Group Development Tools
Practitioners Can Use"
(Minahan and Hutton), 20, 87
groups
assessment of, 85, 88–90
communication skills needed by,
80–85
development of, stages of, 77–79,
85–87, 91
knowledge needed by, 75–80
work, how to structure, 79–80

work-style preferences/tensions,
77, 88–90
groups, qualities of high-performing
description of, 10–15
feedback, 15–17
scaled group inventory, 15–16, 21
self-assessment inventory, 16–17,
22–23
groupthink, 104–105
Group Work Structures, 31, 92–93
growth, shift from quick fix to
continuous growth, 9–10

# H

Herman, J., 61
Hutton, C., 20, 87
hypotheses, generating, 43

# I

improvement, shift from mandated
to motivated, 9
informational altitudes, 60, 61, 71
inquiries
communication skill, 83–84, 99
crafting, 42–43
data dimensions, 60–62
spirit of, 12
intellectual hang time, 30
intervention planning template (IPT),
115–118, 123
interviews, 63
intonation/voice, 99
Iowa State University Extension, 121
Isaacs, D., 110

# J

Janis, I., 96–97, 98

# K

knowledge, needed by groups, 75–80
knowledge delivery to knowledge
construction, shift from, 8–9

# S

satisficing, 97
scaled group inventory, 15–16, 21
scaled surveys, 64
scatter plots, 67
Schein, E. H., 104–106
Schutz, W., 87
Schwarz, R., 84
self-assessment inventory, 16–17,
    22–23
self-authorization, 104–105
self-talk, 100, 101
Simon, H., 97
skills, needed by groups, 80–85
SMART goals, 36, 114–115, 120–121
Spend-a-Buck, 111–112
storming, 78, 79
summative assessment/data, 56
surveys, 63, 64, 72–73
syntax, 99–100

# T

tables, 67
talking skills. *See* communication
    skills
task-relationship, 77
temporal dimension, 60
TimerTools, 38
time without tools, 2
Trends in International Mathematics
    and Science Study (TIMSS), 60,
    61
triangulation, 58–59, 68–69
trust, relational, 13–14
trustworthiness, 57
Tuckman, B. W., 78, 97, 98
Tufte, E., 70

# U

unanimous consent, decision making
    by, 106
unscaled surveys, 64

# V

validity, 56, 57–58
Vogt, E. E., 110
voice, 99

# W

whisker plots, 67
wide-angle questions, 61, 62
Wiliam, D., 56
Winters, L. S., 61
World Café model, 110
Workshop Exercises, 87
workspace design, 31
work-style preferences, 77, 88–90

### Data Dynamics
*Edie L. Holcomb*

Examine the ways your school can better use student achievement data, nonacademic student data, staff data, and parent/community data to identify areas for improvement. Designed to help administrators and leaders, this book also details how teachers can use good data to monitor and motivate students.

**BKF424**

### Data-Based Decision Making
*Edie L. Holcomb*

You're ready to start collecting school data, but what data? How will you find it, and how will you use it once you have it? An informative resource for elementary school principals, this book takes an in-depth look at best data collection practice for schoolwide improvement.

**BKF469**

### More Than a SMART Goal
*Anne E. Conzemius and Terry Morganti-Fisher*

Successful school-improvement efforts not only set SMART goals, but also align them to the school-improvement process, curriculum, instruction, assessment practices, mandates, and professional development. Understand how to properly use the SMART goal process to effect change.

**BKF482**

### Working With Difficult & Resistant Staff
*John F. Eller and Sheila A. Eller*

Identify, confront, and manage all of the difficult and resistant staff you encounter. This book will help school leaders understand how to prevent and address negative staff behaviors to ensure positive school change.

**BKF407**

## Solution Tree | Press
*a division of*
Solution Tree

Visit solution-tree.com or call 800.733.6786 to order.